THE ART OF RECLAIMING YOUR INTENTION & POWER

ACCORDING TO ABRAM THE MAYAN SHAMAN

BY TOM AND SUE MASSARI

Copyright © 2014 by Tom and Sue Massari

ISBN 978-0-7414-9679-9

Printed in the United States of America

Published March 2014

"The Principles of Manifesting: Think It, See It, Form It, Attract It, Become It, Allow It, Act It" is the trademarked property of Tom and Susanna Massari and Oppozatti Productions, Inc.

INFINITY PUBLISHING
1094 New DeHaven Street, Suite 100
West Conshohocken, PA 19428-2713
Toll-free (877) BUY BOOK
Local Phone (610) 941-9999
Fax (610) 941-9959
Info@buybooksontheweb.com
www.buybooksontheweb.com

ACKNOWLEDGEMENTS

Thank you Abram for your loving support and encouragement.

Cover Design by Jan Drozd

Thank you to our good friend and exceptional graphic artist Jan Drozd.

http://www.jfdrozd.com

CONTENTS

QUOTES

"All that a man achieves and all that he fails to achieve is the direct result of his own thoughts. In a justly ordered universe, where loss of equipoise would mean total destruction, individual responsibility must be absolute. A man's weakness and strength, purity and impurity, are his own, and not another man's; they are brought about by himself, and not by another; and they can only be altered by himself, never by another. His condition is also his own, and not another man's. His suffering and his happiness are evolved from within. As he thinks, so he is; as he continues to think, so he remains."

— James Allen

As A Man Thinketh

"One cannot consent to creep when one has an impulse to soar."

— Helen Keller

"Life isn't about finding yourself. Life is about creating yourself."

— George Bernard Shaw

"The purpose of life, after all, is to live it, to taste experience to the utmost, to reach out eagerly and without fear for newer and richer experiences."

— Eleanor Roosevelt

"Imagination is more important than knowledge. Knowledge is limited. Imagination encircles the world."

— Albert Einstein

INTRODUCTION

U niversal wisdom is all knowledge and thought that is available to everyone at any time. From the beginning of man, civilizations and indigenous peoples throughout the world have discovered, expressed, and echoed ancient knowledge through experience, beliefs, myths, storytelling, and ceremonies. While the ideas and practice of positive thinking and the power of thought are nothing new, we present a fresh and interesting approach that is easily understood and can be applied anywhere by anyone at any time.

This information comes from the loving perspective of a non-physical personality named Abram. With his unique and masterful way of delivering this ageless information, he will give you a strong foundation of encouragement as he guides you through visualizations and exercises that will give you insights into human consciousness, the consciousness of the universe, energy, creating and manifesting reality, and how you are intimately connected with all people, nature, and our universe.

Abram's wisdom will subtly take you more deeply into popular spiritual teachings and information about creating and manifesting, and if practiced and applied consistently, you will gain tools useful in everyday life and you will have a greater awareness and understanding of the nature of reality. Every chapter is vibrant and complete with valuable insights into the law of attraction, how to apply the law of attraction, and the laws of the universe.

In Chapter 11, The Principles of Manifesting, he gives a specific step-by-step guide on how to manifest whatever it is you would like to create in your life and reality. He gently takes you through his method of seven steps that begins with a *clear* thought about what you desire, explains when to have reaction to it, when to give your desire reason and meaning, and when to bring in your emotion to charge your desire or goal.

Take the journey of expanded awareness to know who you truly are and what you truly can be. Through his insight of consciousness and the multidimensional aspects of the self, along with his simple, easy and effective visualization exercises, a door has been opened for you to connect with the larger, more complete person you really are.

We offer a new way to connect with yourself, to utilize all of your personal power to create a magnificent life for yourself, and to connect with your greatness. Abram offers ways of reclaiming what is rightfully yours—the right to be happy, successful, and the understanding that you are the grand creator and co-creator of your own life.

The universe is designed to give you everything you wish for, everything you believe in, and everything you want. It is designed for you to create and construct your personal experiences by using your energy, imagination, and beliefs. The consciousness of the universe, and all facets of it, is life. This life force is called by many names: God, Creator, Infinite Intelligence, All That Is, and so on.

By taking a journey within, you can find the answer to every question you have. All experiences are created to serve us, and there can be great freedom in taking responsibility for creations and choices that are made on a daily basis. The intention of this book is to empower.

You hold the key, we just show you where the door is.

In an attempt to keep Abram's information as authentic as possible and with little editing, you will find fractured sentences and repetitiveness in Abram's speech and delivery. This is Abram's style. He repeats himself to emphasize his information so it will be more deeply received by the conscious mind. The content of this book as well as the forthcoming books in "The Art Of" series are all drawn from Abram sessions recorded and documented since 1974.

Tom Massari, the voice for Abram, lived, breathed, and dreamed of a life as a musician knowing that his passion for music would be his path and journey in life. There was no other option for him. Moving to Los Angeles from Chicago in 1971 seemed like the next logical step to further his career, but little did he know just how quickly he would be plucked from the life he knew as a drummer, into a life where a nonphysical entity would choose him to be his voice. Tom had little time or interest for anything psychic, so you can imagine his astonishment when events started to unfold for him over the years that completely altered the course of his life and way of thinking.

Abram's purpose in being with us is to guide us in finding the source of our creativity within and how to express that creative source. His teachings tell us that reality is only an illusion, and that we can change reality with our emotional expression, the choices that we make, and intention. Everything can change when we allow it, and he shows us how to change emotional patterns so we are never stuck in any one pattern of action or reaction. He has an extraordinary sense of humor and loves to play and have fun with us.

We wish you much joy as you consider the wisdom of Abram and apply it to your own life.

A Welcome from Abram in his own words:

Hello my friends,

It is good to be with you. My purpose in being with you physicals is to show you how to cherish your life, how to appreciate all the beauty of life and how to KNOW once you find your own faith within.

There are times during your life when it seems as though an outside influence is forcing you to act or react in certain ways, and in doing so, you are only losing sight of your own action that you are taking. Your reality exists in many varied forms, and when you are *realizing* your action you are *commanding* your reality to be in full force, working for you and not against you. Losing sight of your activeness will bring about the issue of self-destruction; because, to be nonfunctional is to literally kill the force that is within you. That force is called the God Force, the Universal Force, or the Life Force.

As I am, I am still in my own states of evolvement. As you physical human beings do what you do to progress throughout your life and throughout your existence, I also do the same. We all do the same. We are all joined together, you know. In many, many ways we are more a part of you, you are more a part of us than you understand and realize.

Now, that is not to say that I am an aspect of Tom. I am my own individualized identity, as you are and as Tom is. This is one of my many, many experiences that allow me to know myself only that much more so that I could move, and have movement within my own being to graduate to higher steps within my own evolutionary state of being.

Also, since I had three physical lives, it is, in a sense a blessing to me to be able to return to this planet Earth and coexist with human beings once again. It is a very nice feeling for me. It is a joy and a thrill for me and it brings to me more vitality within my own being. And one more thing—I simply enjoy it!

I was alive in the flourishing time of the Mayan Civilization. My role in that life was as a healing man, a magical man, and as I was a Mayan, my name was Kumeh Quey. In my adult day, I stood approximately six-feet-seven inches tall. Clothing consisted of leg coverings, what you would call trousers nowadays—white. What you would call sandals on my feet. On top of the leg coverings would be what you would call a skirt—a white wraparound from the waist to three quarters down to the knee. Top covering, or shirt, would be very loose fitting white material; different styles as you would say, so there was not just one style. Also, a white headband approximately two inches tall. Now, when ceremonies were done, the dress would be all black. Everyday would be all white. As for my head and my face—black, thick, straight long hair down to my shoulders. Somewhat of a squared jaw, high cheekbones, slender face, slender body also, you know. Nose was rather big but slim, not wide. In the middle of the nose was a pronounced bone, not very, but pronounced enough to notice it, you know. Eyes slightly deep set, ears normal, eyebrows somewhat straight across the forehead.

My life in the time of Jesus the Christ was most influential. I sought truth. I gained truth. In that lifetime, I was also known as Abram. My role in that life was as a shoemaker. The main issue from that lifetime, for me alone, was to know of the inner self. How to find love, how to become love, how to embrace life and how not to look down upon life as being somewhat of a curse.

I was also alive and well upon the Continent of Atlantis. My role then was as a Marshall, a Marshall in the 'Force' that was to oversee all the people. After time, I grew tired of being a Marshall, walked away and became a hermit. I learned how to follow rules and how to obey. I also learned that to obey is not everything in life. To obey will only kill what is within one's soul.

In this time, people have been told, are being told, will continue to be told how to live, how not to live, how to think, what to think, what not to think, what clothes to wear, how healthy or sick they will be. Most people, not all, most people become spiritless, robotic people. Now, they have just, and only, misplaced the trust in themselves. Being told all of these things over and over again, people have just lost sight of their own intuitive power and how they can create, recreate, and keep recreating their reality to be just the way they want it to be. I have told people many, many times, over and over again, it takes one person to change the entire planet earth. One person only. So, all things begin within the individual, and all things end within the individual also, you know. People need to hear again, and over and over again all about their own power to change, structure, restructure, create, and recreate their life, lifestyle, and entire reality.

Intention is the key. What you intend, will be. Too many people at this point in time have just set aside and lost sight of their inner power to create and recreate their life, lifestyle, and reality, and this is all about breaking through *all* limitations, because everything, everything is a limitation when it is allowed to be. Also, at the same time, everything can be a freedom when it is allowed to be. When you have intention, the intention creates the power that is needed to create *from* that intention, the entire structure for one's lifetime. So, when you have intention and you set down your intention, that intension will create the power, the vitality, that you need to create what you want in your life. Very simple.

People have been taught throughout their entire lifetime. So, what people need to do, is un-train themselves and retrain themselves by giving up everything they have learned and begin brand new, recreating everything brand new, and this is an easy thing to do, my friends. It does not take work, it is not hard, it can be quick, and simple and easy, but people need to hear that it is all right to change, and they have to give themselves permission to change also, you know.

Thank you my friends.

The Tom and Sue Massari Story

It is undeniably clear that the universe has had a grand purpose for Tom and Sue Massari not only as individuals, but also as a married couple thirty-five years after their first meeting. Their romance that began in 1973 transitioned in that same year and led them to lose contact only to be reunited in 2008. Their relationship today has blossomed into a spectacular partnership on many levels, and the high caliber of writing, speaking, and audio production they are doing is a testament to years of refinement and seasoning.

It was 1971, at the age of twenty-three, when Tom moved to Los Angeles from his native Chicago, with his band, Crucible. An award winning rock and roll drummer, Tom eventually settled in Simi Valley.

Soon after moving into his home, he knew there was definitely a presence in one of the bedrooms, something he could "feel" but not see.

Everything changed for Tom the night of November 3, 1972, while a friend was visiting on vacation. That night, Tom suggested everyone go into the bedroom and try to communicate with the presence. They did not know what they were doing and they certainly were not prepared for what was to happen. Tom and the group began by asking questions such as, who are you? What are you doing here? How did you die? Shortly, the answers to their questions began coming to Tom. He did not hear the answers with his ears, but rather, Tom felt them inside of his body.

When everyone began feeling nauseated and experienced heaviness in their chests, they returned to the front room to relax. Tom went to the kitchen, and as he began to join the others he was stopped in his tracks. He could not move. Electricity was all around and in his body, and he told them something was happening and to watch him to make sure he was all right. Suddenly, this presence began reciting Shakespeare through Tom with an English accent. For about three hours, this other personality would recite Shakespeare for a few minutes, and for a few minutes Tom would snap back to being himself.

Unknowingly to Tom at the time, this paranormal experience was his first introduction to being a channel. The personality gave the name John Rolfes, and said that he lived in England in the late 1700's and was a Shakespearean actor. Driven to investigate, Tom researched John Rolfes at the library and found that he did indeed exist. Tom came across the name *John Rolfes, Shakespearean actor of the late 1700's.* Tom knew that everything about his experience was real. Not being afraid of what had happened, he knew that if it happened again, he would see what developed. Well, it did happen again, and again, and again.

By 1973, through a string of interesting events, Tom found himself back in the Midwest, living in Milwaukee, Wisconsin, where his life took another surprising and unexpected turn. Because of his experience in California with the spirit of John Rolfes, he became involved in metaphysics and opened the Parapsychology Center where ESP development, hypnosis, and meditation were taught. This is when Tom first met Sue.

Shortly after Sue and Tom began dating, someone else manifested through him and gave the name Abram, whom Tom and Sue later discovered was a powerful Mayan shaman. For almost two weeks he would appear to Tom at night in his bedroom. One evening while Tom was teaching an ESP class, Abram's energy came in and filled the room. Sue remembers Tom backing himself into a corner, pushing some metal fold-up chairs out of the way in the process. She could see the energy all around Tom reaching out about three to four feet from his body. Sue recalls Tom's body stiffening and his face contorting. Boisterously, Abram announced himself and began speaking for the first time.

Tom began being a Voice for Abram on a regular basis, although it took him eight years to learn how to "get himself out of the way" so Abram could manifest clearly through him. Very few people in the world were channeling at this time and there was no one to assist Tom. He knew that he was on the right track when one of his California clients, who was a doctor working with a multiple sclerosis patient and having poor results, asked for help. After Abram's advice, the doctor reported that his patient was responding and improving very quickly. It was then Tom knew how valuable Abram's information was and to trust everything that was given him.

In the name of healthy skepticism, mostly his own, Tom allowed himself to be tested by nurses, doctors, ministers, psychiatrists, and psychologists during those earlier years and they all agreed upon one thing. This was real.

Tom returned to Los Angeles, cultivating a large following with his work with Abram and their metaphysical classes. Twenty years later he relocated to Phoenix where he funneled his creativity into acting and composing music. Sue found her way back to her native state of Florida, taking her psychic and mediumship abilities to a professional level in 2003.

In spite of Tom and Sue being out of contact for so many years, they both continued on their independent paths of learning, that has prepared them for their work together today. At the time of their reunion, the pair were in perfect timing to begin their higher purposes as a couple. Tom joined Sue in Florida where they have worked as a team ever since.

Given that Sue was on scene from the start of Tom channeling Abram, it is no surprise that she has been instrumental in helping Tom turn hours and hours of Abram lectures into a compelling series of books called **"The Art Of"** series **According To Abram**, which is making a substantial impact on new and existing fans of Abram around the world. Today, this wisdom is more relevant than ever and can be instrumental in helping men, women, and children have joy-filled lives.

Chapter 1

BREAKING THROUGH LIMITATIONS

Why do you think that you, from time to time, have a hard time dealing with manifesting the reality you want? If you really think about the ideas you have been taught from an early age, you will see why you, and most other people, have a hard time creating the life one wants. You have been taught limitation and fear by nearly everyone around you from birth.

Everywhere you look, everywhere you turn, everything you do, every action you take, everyone you meet, everyone you talk to, brings you into contact with the idea that you and life are limited. We all have limitations imposed upon us by others everyday. Most of the time, we do this through our interactions with others and the relationships we form with others, however brief. Everyone has their own beliefs and perceptions about life and experience, and we pass on and pass down our beliefs. Usually, the opinions and teachings of others are offered to us as well-meaning intentions and most people don't realize they have been taught that life is limited. They don't understand they truly can create what they want in life. The truth is, you can create your own reality and have it be exactly as you want it to be.

What does the idea and experience of limitation do to you? It immediately takes you out of the realm of creative functionality and places you into a situation of guarding yourself. You begin guarding what you do, guarding how you do what you do — worrying about the result of what you do, how you are doing it, and worrying that it will all turn out to be less than what you want it to be. Other people's limiting beliefs may cause you to question yourself and your abilities.

> **Looking at limitation, you will come to understand and realize that limitation is simply fear.**

From birth, your parents have placed limitations upon you, believing they were being loving and protective by teaching you proper values and behaviors. Even your friends have unwittingly placed limitations on you. When parents, friends, teachers, spiritual leaders, or anyone is talking to you about their own experiences and limitations, they are introducing their energy into your reality. Life is energy, and we exchange energy with everything and everyone we come into contact with. We cannot help but exchange and feed off of each other's energy — it is a natural part of life. Over time though, and with enough consistency, the energy of your friends, teachers, parents, and the limitations of others may influence you and that influence becomes the energy of your limitations also. People trade their beliefs and attitudes back and forth by talking about them with one another. People can also trade their freedoms back and forth simply by talking to one another *about* freedoms and possibilities. In schools and churches you are taught limitation, and you are taught to know your limits, to follow the rules, to fit in, and believe and not question those things that are contained in the books given to you to read whether or not they are holy books or text books. Depending on an individual's belief system, one may be taught there is only one right answer and one right way to solve a problem, when people intuitively sense this isn't the truth. There are many ways to find answers and solve problems if one is given the freedom to explore options and do things his or her own way, but there are many times people are taught that options are limited. The message is to be normal and to do as everyone else does. Live and believe like the majority, and don't rock the boat and do things the accepted way.

The truth is, you have the innate ability and freedom to create. You have *always* had the freedom to create, but often you have lost sight of that freedom. Your parents, your schooling, your religious teachings, and all the rest, set up major limitations for you with a "one-size-fits-all" mentality. How many times have you heard words like these? "Don't act that way." "Don't say that." "Do things this or that way." "That won't work." "That is impossible." "The idea is ridiculous." "No one else has ever done that, so what makes you think you can?" You shouldn't... You have too... You must... You can't..."

Everything you do has a limit or limitation placed upon it—everything. How you think, how you speak, the words you use, and the actions you take. Most of the time, your reactions will limit you, because when you react to something, it is usually of a negative nature. That in itself is limiting. Your negative energy will limit your freedom functionality or your "free functionality." Looking at limitation, you will eventually come to understand and realize that limitation is simply fear.

Fear

Fear comes in many ways and in many disguises and varieties. You might have fear of success, fear of failure, or fear of the unknown. Fear of rejection is a powerful one. Think about how many times during your lifetime you have felt rejected by something or someone. You are met with rejection on a daily basis, and I would bet you have experienced rejection so many times that you have lost count. By this time you really should be, or can be, numb to the idea of rejection. By being numb, I mean that by now, at this point in your life, rejection should mean nothing to you. Often though, you get used to something so much that it becomes a pattern. So, let's think about and explore the pattern of rejection.

Fear of Rejection

Rejection comes in many forms, and when it comes right down to it, being rejected can hurt because people have a desire to be accepted. Yet, you meet with rejection repeatedly throughout your lifetime and you are still alive and still functional. You are still functioning—right? Also, when you want to be, you are still brilliant. All the times you have had rejection placed upon you in your life, really, really, really means nothing. When someone rejects or discourages you, the person is only speaking his or her belief about his or her own self. Think about how often you have heard negative words about wasting your time on something, or remarks about something that has already been done, or someone saying that "they" would never do that. Since those other people would never do that, whatever "that" may be, they are voicing their lack of faith in themselves and attempting to place their limitations on you to limit your actions. They believe if they cannot do something, you cannot do it either. They cannot see beyond their own limited thinking. In most cases this is done purely on a subconscious level, and usually, people will deny their own motives, because people are not aware of their own emotionality or they are disconnected from it.

Sometimes people will play the devil's advocate and have reasons why your idea won't work, or people close to you will find ways of sabotaging your efforts, because they don't want you to change or do something outside their own idea of who you are. If you change, or your efforts are successful, it changes their world too—and some people like the status quo. Many people fear change, so they play it safe by repeating the same, dull, boring things they find safe and familiar. They cannot imagine you breaking free, because subconsciously it frightens them. If you change, they might have to change too to continue having you in their lives. Your actions may cause them to question their own lives and beliefs, and that can be very frightening for those who fear change.

> **People will reject you because you don't align with their system of belief. They use you as a reflection of their own self.**

Many people will reject you because you don't align or agree with their system of belief. What they are really doing is rejecting themselves, and they use you as a reflection of their own self. Yes, you are a reflection of them, but you are also *you*. You are your own unique, creative, brilliant being. Depending on your own situation, what you can do—and in some cases, what you need to do—is remove yourself from everyone else's belief systems and begin to *recreate* your own unique belief system. Why? Because at this point, you are a culmination of your life experiences, and that includes everyone else's systems of beliefs and ideas—everything that you have rejected or held on to. How can you not be? It is all you have been taught since birth.

If your life is not going the way you want it to, it is time to break free of the limiting beliefs you have been taught and now believe in, and form your own new truths. It is time to express your own freedom, creativity, and unique self. It is time to let go of and shed old stories.

You Can Choose to Break Free

You truly can remove yourself from the belief systems you have created for yourself and of others and begin to create, or recreate, your own unique belief system, if you want to. When you do this, you will find something taking place. You will find that all those people who have been rejecting you may fall away from your life and your reality. Maybe you have friends that you have known for a long time, but once you begin to create, or recreate your own unique belief system, they will fall away from your life and you will lose them as friends. For you, this can be a very good thing.

What is the definition of a friend? A friend is someone or something that is willing to support you emotionally, creatively, and spiritually. People who love you want to see you happy and successful, and will not feel they are in competition with you. They will support you and not drag you down. A true friend isn't someone who wants to influence you to take on their beliefs and conform to their expectations. There is an old saying that you can count the number of your true friends on one hand — friends you will have for a lifetime. You will meet many people during your lifetime, and you will think many of them are your friends. Are they really, or do they just need to have you around to feed their own limiting belief systems?

I am not trying to belittle you or the friends you have in your life. I am simply suggesting that you look at yourself for a time. Let go of everything and everyone, and take some time for yourself, and either create or recreate your belief system. Focus on you. What would you like your beliefs to be and to be all about? Who, and how, do you want to be? Create that in your life. Once you begin doing that, you will see that many people who have been around you will fade away. They will fall away, either for good, or they may leave your life for a while, and then find their way back another time. This falling away can be a good thing.

During your life, people come in and out, in and out, in and out of your life, and many times you will create people, and create the foundation and opportunity for certain people to be in your life, in your reality for a time, to serve you. You will create them to serve you, because you create everything in your life—everything in your reality is here to serve you. Once you start your restructuring process and you find yourself minus a few, or many, people you have known for a long time, don't feel sorry for yourself. See this as an opportunity. See it as an opportunity to move on, to restructure your life the way you want it to be. Focus on what you want to do, how you want to do it, and simply—Do It. Do it YOUR way.

So, you begin changing things and you are excited and enthusiastic, and someone gives you the message that they don't approve, or they somehow throw a monkey wrench into the mix. Again, you are getting a negative response. You've probably been called stupid a few times in your life whether by tone of voice, joke, body language, or blatantly. What is stupid? What is stupidity? Does stupidity really have a meaning? If you look at the word, it is stupid in itself. It is a silly thing. It is simply a judgment that someone will place upon you.

Any time someone tells you that you can't do something, or that your ideas or actions won't work, they are just reminding themselves that they cannot do it, or they don't want you to do something better than them. They use you to reflect back to them all that they cannot do, or haven't done themselves. Who really is to say you can't do it? Maybe they can't do it. Let them have that experience. It is their right. At the same time, you have your experience in a different way, and that is your right.

When Things Go Awry, Try Them A Different Way

Now, speaking of experience, often you will begin something, and the experience of the thing itself and what you want to create will judge you. It will reject you. You will meet with rejection from what you are trying to do — from the experience of what you are trying to do. Things will just not be working out the way you wanted them to work out. Why would this happen to you?

Reality is here to serve you.

Look at your own beliefs about yourself. What are they? What are your beliefs about your ability to do what you want to do in any way you want to do it? Do you really deserve everything? Do you have a fear of deserving everything?

Many people do have a fear of deserving everything. Why do you think people would fear they deserve everything? It is because of old stories and domestication that is deeply ingrained from early training. "This isn't the way you should be." "You shouldn't deserve everything." "How can you deserve everything?" "Know your limits." "Know your limitations." "There is no way in the universe you are worthy of everything." This is what you have been taught and have learned, one way or another, throughout your life.

Just by being a physical human being, alive, well, and breathing, is proof that you DO deserve everything. You are divinely created and born into possibility. Reality is here to serve you. You don't need a reason to be deserving of everything life has to offer. You ARE life. You simply DO deserve everything. So, when you are doing something, and the situation of what you are doing seems to go awry, don't take it personally. Don't see it as an attack upon you, or think that something is wrong with you. It is not.

Everything is energy and every event has its own timing. Maybe the energy of what you are trying to do is just not aligned properly. If you have an idea and things aren't working out your way, take the same idea and use it in a slightly different way.

Let's say you would like to do something or have something, it can be anything, any idea. If you think about it, you will realize there are many ways to use that idea, not just one way. There are many ways to do the same thing — many different ways. If what you are trying to do is not working, don't reject yourself. This is something people do to themselves all the time. DON'T JUDGE YOURSELF. Simply know the energies of what you are trying to do are just not aligning properly. Think of other ways to use the same idea, and use it in a slightly different way. Then you will find the idea will work for you. Sometimes timing is everything.

Be in A State of Creative Functionality

Think about how many times things *do* work for you. Do you think things work for you when you let them work for you? What do you think happens when you do let things work for you? *How* do you let things work for you? When you are letting things work for you, you are not thinking of rejection, judgment, or whether you deserve something or not, and there is not a thought of whether you can accomplish your goal or not. You are simply in a mode of creativity and creative functionality.

When I say creative functionality, I don't mean you have to be an Einstein when you are trying to do something, even though you are. Frankly, many people are beyond being an Einstein. I simply mean, when you are in a mode of creative functionality, you are focused upon what you want to do, and you are completely focused upon doing it. This is creative functionality—doing what you want to do, no holds barred. You will find there is nothing in your way, because you are not entertaining the idea, or even slightly considering anything being in your way.

11

Often it is not others who reject you. It is *you* rejecting yourself. You may have many reasons and excuses to not do something, and this is how you reject yourself and your ideas. "Well, this has already been done. It probably won't sell. I don't know how to market my idea. I would love to do that, but it takes money, and I don't have the money."

These are limitations you are placing on yourself. MONEY IS ONLY AN IDEA. IT IS A FORM OF ENERGY. You may be stopping yourself because of that excuse. It is an excuse, a limitation. Limitations are excuses to keep you in a comfort zone when you refuse to stretch yourself to really do what you want to do. You are keeping yourself safe. "Well, this is comfortable and I'm used to it. If I take myself out of my comfort zone, I'll meet with rejection ... and all the rest." So, you limit yourself. Other grand excuses and limitations you use without realizing what you are doing are, "Gee, I don't know enough—I would love to be that, or do that, but I don't know enough, or how to do it—I can't do it without more schooling or training."

This is not a personal attack upon you. This is simply to point out what most people do every day. If you look within yourself, with no judgment, you will find that maybe you *do* know what you need to do and how to do it. You *do* know what you need to know to do anything. If you look within yourself, you will find this to be true.

Here is one more grand limitation you place upon yourself, and this is a big one. "Why even try? It won't work, I've tried it before and it hasn't worked out. It won't work out, I know it. I just know it. It really won't work out, I know it."

It won't work out, because you know it won't work out—but what if you knew it *might* work out? It just might. Wouldn't it change your way of thinking about the idea? Of course it would. "Well, if it might work out, then I might be able to do it."

In thinking this way, in a more positive way, you will find something taking place within you, and this will be a slight excitement about what you would like to do. "It just might work out. Let me see, if I do it this way, it has a very good chance of working out. If I do it that way, it has an even better chance of working out. If I just dive in and do it, I can't fail. I can't miss. It will be a hit."

Thinking this way, you are finely focused upon and within your freedom to create. You are not considering, you are not in consideration of, you are not allowing into your being, into your life, and into your reality—the idea of limitation. A limitation is something you allow and give permission to, to prevent you from being you. Let me repeat that. *A limitation is something you allow and give permission to, to prevent you from being you.*

How many times have you compared yourself to someone else? When you do this, you are telling yourself that you don't have what you want. You don't have things, and if you had what he has, what she has, then you would feel good about yourself. You would be equal. Why must you have some "thing" to feel good about yourself? If you felt good about yourself for no reason at all, then you would have everything.

Why? Because when you feel good about yourself, you are not allowing limitation into your reality, because you are not even considering limitation. You are feeling good about yourself, and when you feel good about yourself, you can do anything. You have done it before. You have had times when you felt very good about yourself—many times—and you have created many brilliant things in your life.

Maybe you can begin thinking of all the things, or a few of the things, or some of the things, or even one of the things you have created for yourself— what you wanted to create, or something you had gotten, something you had created, or something you had manifested. When you are thinking of that thing—or those things, or all of them, or some of them, or many of them—think about how you were feeling at the time. You were feeling—and I will guarantee you—you were feeling very good about yourself, and you were in your own freedom. You were not considering limitations.

Limitations are excuses that you use to keep yourself in your comfort zone. Many times, you have a fear of looking silly to someone else. "If I do this, and I really would like to do it, I might look silly. So maybe, I'll tone it down and do it just a little bit, and just to a slight degree. Then I won't look so silly."

What makes you think you will look silly? So what? What makes you think that way? Think about it for a time. What makes you think you will look silly? What makes you think anyone will reject you if you are not rejecting yourself? You know by now, if you are not rejecting yourself, if you are not judging yourself, no one can, or will, reject or judge you, because everything begins within you — and so does limitation.

> **Limitations are excuses you use to keep yourself in your comfort zone. Many times, you limit yourself because you have a fear of looking silly to someone else.**

The structure of your educational system teaches you to limit yourself in school and to follow the rules. You are under the influence of your teachers, school district, city, state, and federal government. The society of school can be cruel and tricky with all the pressures young people face, yet some kids have a wonderful school experience, while for others, school can be very torturous. You created your school. You created your experience. Your education or your lack of one is your reality. You create everything. Even before you were born, you created and set up your experiences and challenges for this life. You created those situations in school that taught you how to be, situations that taught you limitations as well as successes. Why would you do that? Think about it for a time.

You Deserve Everything

Why do you have a need to create limitation for yourself? Could it be to keep yourself safe, comfortable, and not at risk? At risk of what? At risk of looking silly? At risk of being rejected or not being accepted? At risk of being beaten down for your ideas? There are no risks at all. *Unless you challenge yourself, there are no challenges in life either.* There are only, and there are just, situations that you will use in one creative way or another, so you can express what is within you.

I'll bet you have something inside of you that is just bursting to come out. Something that you want, or want to do, or a way you would like to be. Something you are just dying to express.

> "I can feel it in my bones. I know I can do that. I know I can be that way. I know I can have that. I know I can do it. I know I can."

Why aren't you doing it?

You may think, "Well, I don't know." As long as you keep saying, "I don't know," you won't know. You won't know anything. You won't know that yes, you can do it. You say you feel you can do it. If you feel and think you can do it, I am telling you, you *can* do it. Maybe it is time to stop saying, "Well, I don't know," and start saying, "Yes, I do know. Yes, I do know. I do know. I DO know I CAN."

How many times during the day do you say, "I can't?" If you really pay attention to your internal dialogue, you will see how many times, and different ways, you say, "I can't." Every time you catch yourself, stop and remind yourself that you can. "Oh, yes I can. What am I saying? Sure I can." Don't say, "Oh, of course I can, stupid me. Of course I can, silly me—I'm just being stupid." Don't

say it that way, because you are limiting yourself
again. You are calling yourself a negative idea—
stupid or silly. When stupid is really stupid in its
own self—it has no meaning. Simply say, "I can.
Yes, I can. I can anything." Because you CAN
anything, if and when you want to.

You skip through your life merrily going your
way and creating limitation after limitation, upon
limitation, upon limitation, and you are doing fine.
Then one day, you stop and think, "What am I
doing? I don't have what I want to have. I haven't
accomplished what I set out to accomplish."

Why? Maybe you are afraid of extending
yourself. Maybe you have a fear of rejection or a fear
of success. Maybe you are afraid of doing something
the wrong way and being ridiculed for it.

Being that you are creative, you will create many
ways to stop yourself. How creative you are! How
brilliant you are! If you can be creative enough to
create ways to stop yourself, imagine what you can
do once you begin creating ways to free yourself—to
free yourself of limitation in any form, in any form at
all. In ANY form. Imagine what you can do.

Stop right now, close your eyes, and simply
imagine what you can do. IMAGINE what you
could do—what you would be able to do if you
simply created freedom. You are most likely
thinking of a few things you could be doing, and
you just might be getting excited about them. If you
are getting excited about them in that short a time,
just thinking about them, think of the excitement
you can have if you begin doing them. Once you do

something with no judgment placed upon yourself, no excuses, and no limitations, and you begin doing things *that* way—you would really see the power that you are and the power that you have. That power is to be anything, to be anyone, to be any way, and to have anything.

If you were to be that way, think of all those people who have been rejecting you, judging you. You could help change their lives also. When they see you doing things nonstop, no holds barred, with nothing in your way, nothing stopping you, they will begin to think that maybe they can be the same way. They will try themselves out, bit by bit, by bit, here and there, just a bit at a time, and eventually they will begin to create freedom also.

Drop all self-judgments and limitations that are upon you—and there are many. Chip away at it. Of course you can be that way. Of course you can do that. Above all, of course you do deserve it. You deserve everything, even if you don't believe it right now. Listen closely, because I am telling you, you DO deserve everything. You are worthy of everything, and you deserve everything, simply because you deserve it. Again, simply because you deserve it. Nothing attached to it. Simply because you deserve it.

You can either skip through your life and go along your merry way, deserving everything, or you can keep yourself safe. If you have to make a choice, if you had to make a choice, if you had to, what would your choice be? Think about it. I would bet many people would keep themselves safe. It is an easy way. It is a very easy way. To begin creating can be the hard way for people who have created a habit of playing it safe in life. It can truly be the hard way. You might have many things standing in your way when you begin creating, and when you begin doing what you want to do. You might have many things standing in your way, but you might not, and if you, and should you, find that you have things standing in your way, SO WHAT! Go around them. Just go around them.

Do not plow through them; they will knock you down. When you fight something, it will fight back. Go around them. Sidestep them. Do something else. Take the idea and work it another way, and you will win, and you will do what you want to do, and you will not have a hard time.

Play Life As A Game

Life CAN be a very, very easy idea. I'll say it again: life CAN be a very, very easy idea. It is only an idea. That is all it is. This reality is only an illusion—even Einstein knew this. Some play a very serious game in life while others play a joyful game. Life *is* a grand game, and this is not to imply frivolousness. Why not see limitation as a game? Play with limitation.

"Well, I'm feeling undeserving today … think I'll play with that one for a time. Hey everyone, I'm undeserving. Yes siree, I *am* undeserving. How about you? Are you undeserving too?"

Play it. Play it as a game. When you play it as a game, it will change the game. It will lose its negative energy and become a positive. You will begin laughing, and you will think, "I'm deserving of everything. This is only and just a game."

With everything you do, visualize and think you *are* doing it, and you will do it, and you have done it brilliantly. "Well, I think I'll have a sandwich today. I'm hungry. I'll eat a sandwich and I won't judge the sandwich. I'll love the sandwich. I won't reject the sandwich, and I'll accept the sandwich because it serves me."

Everything you do, play it as a game. When you play it as a game, you have no judgment and you have no limitation. If you do, remember limitation is also a game. Play it as a game. You don't have to set yourself up for limitation. You don't have to do that. *Start living what you want to create.*

So, you might have a fear of something. Think about why you might have that fear. When you have time, think about why you might have fear — fear of doing something, fear of being a certain way, fear of accomplishing something. No matter what the fear is all about, you have a fear. Everyone has fears, even if they don't admit to it. Why do you have fear? When you begin to think about it, you might discover the only reason you have fear is because you have not yet done what you would like to do. You really don't know how things are going to go if you begin to do them. The only way to find out how it will go is to simply DO IT. *Fear is only an idea.*

Define failure. "If I really look at failure, it's also a success, because it teaches me not to do it again, or to do it another way. There's always something to be learned from failure."

Precisely. If nothing else, failure will teach you to not do it again the same way. I really want to drive this home to you — *take the same idea and do something in a slightly different way using the same idea, and it will work for you.*

It is important that you understand that the energies need to line up, to align themselves properly, in order for anything to become manifest in reality. The energies must be aligned in your reality. They must also be aligned in your body. You must have balance within you. With balance, you will not have illness. If you are imbalanced, you will have illness. When you correct the imbalance and become balanced again, the illness will go away. Balance your reality and your reality's illness will go away. Balance the ideas of what you want to do, and they will manifest themselves, and rejection will go away. Limitation will go away. It is all a matter of balance. This may include a long-term illness where someone will use his or her entire life to create a balance.

The Feeling of Freedom

At this point, I would like you to think about one thing that you would really like to do. Not a way you would like to be, but one thing you would like to do. Not something you would like to have, but one thing you would really, really like to do. See yourself doing it — laughing while you are doing it — having fun while you are doing it. As you are doing this, see it working out precisely the way you want it to.

This is the feeling of freedom. You are in the experience of having no limitation. You are free, you are easy, you are feeling good about everything, and what you want to do is working out your way.

Now, I want you to think of something else you would really like to do. Think of that one thing and see everything going wrong with that one thing. See everything going wrong. Now you are in the experience of judgment, limitation, and failure. Since you are in the experience of failure, how did everything going wrong serve you? How does seeing everything going wrong serve you? How does all that judgment, limitation, and failure feel to you? I'll bet it showed you that you weren't allowing yourself the magic you have within you, and that magic is to have faith in yourself and the universe. I would also bet it was showing you there is a different way to do things, and I'll bet it was showing you that you were taking yourself out of the idea of timing.

"Well, I have this idea. I would like to do this. I would like to do that, but it will take quite a while — ten years, five years, three months, or maybe not until tomorrow."

You are limiting yourself again. You are introducing another limitation. It is one more excuse for you to keep yourself in your comfort zone. Why would something take five years to manifest for you?

"Well, because I don't have the money ..."

Here we go again. *Money is an idea.* It is only energy. It is a game. What other excuses might you have to let your idea wait five years, ten years, or tomorrow, or three months, or two months, or next week? What other excuses can you think of?

"Well, I guess you've got me there. I have no other excuses. I suppose I'll go and create it right now."

Human beings are one thing and that one thing is *power.* You have the power to be free, to be creative, to be brilliant, to be magnificent, to have everything, and to have it all your way. This means achieving it by living in your truth and your own brilliance. Not stepping on others or getting what you want in an unethical way. You can always make that choice though.

> **Life can be a very, very easy idea.
> Life is a game. Why not have
> limitation be a game? Play with
> limitation and it will lose its
> negativity and become positive.**

You also have the power to create limitation upon limitation upon limitation, in a very brilliant way. Think about how you would really like to be. Take a bit of time. Take three weeks time to think about it, and I mean to really think about how you would like to be. Don't rush it along.

"Well, I don't need three weeks time. I know right now how I would like to be."

Well, I suggest you take three weeks time and think about it. Think about how you would like to be for three weeks. Know what? I guarantee you one thing. If you do that, in three weeks time you will find yourself being how you would like to be, doing what you would like to do, and being rewarded for doing and being it. Guaranteed.

So now what? Will you create other limitations you haven't yet thought of, or will you simply turn your focus to other things, like freedom, being functional, and taking action in a positive way? Make your choice and DO IT. Taking yourself out of your comfort zone is a blessing. It is a very good thing. It is a freedom. Maybe it is something you haven't really, truly, completely experienced in your lifetime. Maybe you have kept yourself in a comfort zone in one way or another way.

Now Is The Time

Now is the time, if you want it to be. Now is the time to break out of your comfort zone. BE what you want to be. BE the way you want to be. DO what you want to do. CREATE what you want to create. HAVE what you want to have—simply because it is your right, and yes, you do deserve it. Nothing is out there to stop you except YOU and the excuses you may tell yourself over and over again. Laugh them away. Simply release and laugh them away. Bid them a fond farewell.

Chapter 2

BRINGING IN THE NEW

B ringing in the new is all about bringing new energies into your body, your consciousness, your spirit, and your reality. It is also about *allowing* the energies into your body, your consciousness, your spirit, and your reality. I say new, because this may be a new experience for you, which will be highly personalized and structured for *you*.

At times, when you bring something to you, you are not *allowing* it to come to you. There is a difference. Many times, when you bring something to you, you look at the *result* of what it can do for you, and you don't recognize the step-by-step process. On the other hand, when you *allow* things come to you, when you *let* something come to you, you embrace it with no expectation at all. You are not looking at the result. You are not pondering or thinking of the final result. You are just enjoying the step-by-step process that it will take itself through so it can manifest fully, totally, and completely for you, within you, or around you. You are in the moment and enjoying the journey.

> **If you really don't know what might happen, how can you fear what you don't yet know? What might happen might be a good thing.**

There are ways of bringing things to you and there are ways of allowing things to come to you. Once you recognize what you would like to have come to you, you can then begin allowing it to come to you. Once you acknowledge a need for something, a need in a positive sense, then you can begin allowing it to come to you. Once you understand what it can do for you, then you can let it come to you. *You might find it hard to recognize something that you need, and bring it to you at the same time.* Many times, when you do that, and function in that way, you just might bring what you want to you with anxiety or desperation.

Desperation Makes Things Work in Reverse

Take a good look at all the things you need in a desperate or anxious way. Think of all those things you *need* in a desperate way, and all those things you can really do without. If, and/or, when you need something in a desperate way, it probably won't be a good thing for you to have that which you need or that which you want. Often, when you go about your day and you are trying to create something in your life or reality, your need comes from desperation or with anxiety. Many times, you won't recognize this because it can be very subtle, and you will create that which you want or need, and it will begin working in reverse for you. It will not work out the way you want it to, or expect it to. It will work out in ways that will try and test you.

Everyone has issues in their life that *try* them. Everyone has trying issues in their life—everyone. You deal with them the best way you know how to at the time, but exactly *how* are you dealing with them at the time? Are you dealing with them with frustration and anxiety, or are you dealing with them in an allowing way? If you are dealing with those issues, those situations, those things, or those people, with anxiety or desperation, then you will only make the situation a bit worse for you—and you should know this by now.

A better way to work with issues that *try* you is to allow the issues to run their course. Step back, step away from the issue or the situation, or the individual, or whatever it might be at the time. Step back. Step away from it and just observe it. Be an objective observer and stay calm. Let it run its course. Let the individual run his or her course also. When the course has been run completely, then what you can do to effectively cause a good outcome for, or with, the issue or the individual, is simply remove it from your reality in a very gentle way by sending it love—not loving it—but sending it love and appreciation. Tell it, it has served its own purpose, but it does not serve you any longer, and simply bid it a pleasant goodbye. This will also work when you want to let go of old stories about yourself.

Giving Yourself Permission For Life To Work For You

Think of an issue that is *trying* in your life right now, and in your imagination see yourself stepping back from that situation or issue. Take yourself out of the emotionality of the situation. Remove yourself emotionally. Don't involve yourself emotionally at all, and just witness the situation that is taking place. See it taking place. Allow it to run its course in your imagination right now, and see it ending right now. Imagine yourself giving it your appreciation, giving it a bit of your love, and telling it to be on its way. Explain to it that it *did* serve itself, but it does not serve you now. It has no purpose being in your life, in your reality, at this time. It is better off elsewhere, and let it go. See it moving away from you.

Now, bring back your emotions. Begin feeling your emotions within you again, and imagine that you are creating a situation in place of the other one—the one you just bid a goodbye to. This new situation will be a situation that you will allow to come to you. You will allow it to come to you. You will allow it to work out in its best way for your highest good. See this taking place right now. You really don't have to do much once you give it permission to work within its own framework for your highest good. It will always work in the best way it can for you at any given point.

Give it permission to work for you. See it taking place right now. Yes, you can now involve yourself emotionally this time. It will be a good thing. Feel its emotions. Feel the emotions of the issue or the situation.

You don't have to send it love or appreciation, because once you give it your permission to work for you, it will realize your appreciation and your love. Then it will become a part of your reality, and it will become a part of you and your identity.

Allow New Energy Into Your Life

There are many things that you let come to you in your life, and sometimes those things don't work. Allow a new energy, right here and right now, to come into your body. Begin to gently, and positively, let a new energy come into your body. Now, listen carefully. You do not have to know what the energy is all about. You do not have to know how it works. All you have to know is that you are giving it permission to come to you. You are ready to embrace a new energy. Put that out into the universe right now. Tell yourself and tell the universe that, yes, you are ready to let a new energy come into your body. Do that right now, and do nothing else for the time being. Just do that much right now.

A Technique to Create A New You

This visualization technique is an excellent way to bring new energy to you. It may be a new experience for you, and what you do with this exercise and the energy it will bring within you is highly personalized and structured just for you, because you will automatically individualize the exercise to fit you.

Imagine at the very top of your head, there is a funnel. The wide mouth is pointing out, away from the top of your head. The small mouth is pointing toward your head, not in your head, but toward your head. Imagine that a new excited and exciting energy is coming into that funnel, and it is forming itself around your body. It is forming itself around your body.

Let yourself feel the excitement of the energy. Feel the energy, feel the excitement in and of the energy all around your body. Once you feel the excitement of and in the energy, let the energy gently settle into the layers of your skin. You might let yourself feel coolness, heat, or a tingling sensation on, or in, your skin. That is all you need to do for right now. Do nothing else. Just let the energy enter into the layers of your skin right now. Do nothing else. Just feel it right now.

As you are doing that, you might have a sense of what the energy is about. You do not need to know what the energy is about or need to know its purpose. It has a definite reason for being ... FOR YOU. It has a definite purpose FOR YOU. It knows what it is doing, because it is and it has a consciousness just like you. It knows what it is doing.

As you are feeling the excitement and the energy in the layers of your skin, just simply let the energy and the excitement melt into every tissue of your body, every bone in your body, in a very gentle way. Feel the energy and feel the excitement coursing through your veins, because it is now in your blood and a part of your blood.

Feel it coursing through your veins, your arteries, and feel it bringing more life to you. Do this now. Do nothing else. Do it right now.

Again, you do not need to know what the energy is all about. You do not need to know. You might have an idea about it, but do not try to figure out the energy. Not yet. Just allow it to settle into every cell in your body. Let it settle in now. Let it settle into every cell in your body—you can feel it and you can see it.

Imagine it taking place right now. You can feel it and you can see it. Feel it coursing through your veins and arteries. Do it right now.

Now, take the next step by imagining that you are turning into this energy. With your eyes closed, using your grand imagination, imagine your entire body turning into this energy. You are becoming this energy. Imagine that you are *becoming* the energy.

Begin feeling emotions taking place inside you. Feel emotions within you. They will probably feel new to you, which is a good thing. This is a very good thing. If they feel brand new to you, allow them. Allow them to stay inside of you. Allow them to reside within you, taking up residence within you. Allow them to become your new state of emotion.

As you are doing this, as you are letting yourself become the energy, you might be feeling the new structure and orientation of emotion within you. Let yourself expand as the new energy. Fill the room you are in, because you *are* ever-expanding energy.

You've become a new identity of energy. You *are* a new being right now. Keep your eyes closed and listen very carefully to me. What you have done so far, and to this point, with this exercise, is you have completely restructured your entire body. You may feel aches and pains leaving. You may feel a brand new vitality. You may feel a brand new strength and a brand new system of health throughout your body. This is what you have done so far with this exercise at this point.

As you are filling the room with yourself, being the energy, imagine the room that you are in brilliantly glowing within you, because you *are* the energy. It is brilliantly glowing in a beautiful golden color within you. It is glowing within you, within your energy, within your new energy. As this is taking place, begin seeing your emotions flying around the room. See them. Allow them to have form. Do this now.

Begin to recognize your emotions and see them flying around the room. Flying all around you. See this taking place. Imagine it taking place, and let the emotions take on their own forms. Give them permission to assume their own forms and they will show themselves to you. Now you understand your emotions in two different ways within you, feeling and seeing them in your imagination. See them flying or floating around, gently in your room, whichever you prefer—flying or floating.

As you are doing all of this, expand yourself a bit more, and then begin to draw all the emotions back within you. Let all the emotions come back to you. Let them come back to you. Do not bring them to you but *allow* them to come back to you.

Simply feel what you have become at this point. Feel what you have become.

If, by some chance you feel nothing, or you feel no change at all, repeat this a few times and you will have beautiful results. If you are feeling brand new, just continue feeling brand new. Feel this new energy inside of you, and feel yourself having become this new energy.

Believe, from this moment on, that you can do anything you want, in any way you want. Listen to your heartbeat. Hear your heartbeat. If you cannot hear it, imagine that you are hearing it. Imagine a heartbeat that you can hear inside of you. You will not hear it with your ears. You will hear it inside of you. Hear your heartbeat inside of you. Hear it within you. This is your life force.

This life force will bring you everything you need from this moment on, to do anything you want, in any way you want. Being this new energy, you will not allow yourself to be as you were, because you are letting go of the old you. You really won't allow yourself to do things in the same old way, because you are a new individual. By being a new individual, you can, and will, only do things in a new way.

Now that you have allowed the energy to come to you, open your eyes and take one deep breath, refresh yourself, and just feel your body. You should be able to feel the bones in your body, the blood coursing through the veins in your body, every cell in your body, and every tissue in your body. There is one more step in this technique, and then we will move on.

Close your eyes and imagine the funnel again. This time, the small mouth is gently inside of your head and it is resting just slightly above your brain. The wide mouth is outside of your head. Imagine the same energy, the same excitement, coming through the funnel and enveloping your entire brain. Do this right now. Do only that. Do nothing else at this point. Feel the energy. Feel the energy surrounding and enveloping your brain. Let the energy into your brain gently. Let the energy melt into your brain gently.

What you are doing is reactivating your entire brain's functionality. From this point on, you should have more clarity in your thinking, in the way you see things, and how you interpret things. New connections are being made between your neurons.

Gently open your eyes. Take a deep breath and refresh yourself. Take a moment to simply feel how you feel. Experience yourself being this new person, this new individual. Experience yourself being this new energetic being.

Repeat this exercise as often as you like to reinforce the new energy.

A Quick Expansion Technique

Think of your reality. Your reality is wherever you are at the time. No matter where you are, that is your reality. Again, *wherever you are, that is your reality*. Whatever you are doing, that is your reality also. Begin thinking of, and considering, your reality. Just consider your reality. It naturally goes beyond your home. Think of the places you are usually in throughout your day, throughout your week, throughout your month, and your year. This is all your reality. Everything is your reality.

Close your eyes and imagine yourself in the room you are in. Imagine yourself in this space. Now imagine your surroundings becoming nonphysical. Imagine, as you are in your room with your eyes closed—close your eyes and imagine the room you are in becoming nonphysical. Let it all fade away and become simply energy. Let the room you are in become nothing more than, nothing less than, energy. Let it lose everything that is physical about its appearance and its being. Imagine your room being nonphysical. This brings to you the opportunity to allow your room, your home, wherever you are at any given moment in time, to become the entire universe.

Open your eyes, take a deep breath, and refresh yourself. The more you do this exercise, the better results you will have.

What The Universal Shift Is All About

Really, you exist in a non-reality. *You think it to be a certain way, and it appears to be that way.* If you were to break down your reality to its most simple form, you would find yourself existing in an energy reality, an energetic reality, with no physical substance at all—none at all. You would find yourself as energy, along with everything and everyone else as energy also. Being that you have let your room, your home, your reality, your environment, become the universe, what you can do right now is begin thinking of the universe changing within its own structure. This is what the grand shift is all about. This is what the shift is *all* about.

The universe is changing within its own structure. It is spiraling through an alternate universe, and by July 17, 2013, it will have completed the shift, at which time all people — ALL people — will have the opportunity to think and to act in a more Christ-like way. This has nothing to do with religion at all. *This has everything to do with elevating your thought pattern and allowing yourself to become what you truly can become and truly be.*

The nature and structure of the universe is a spiral itself, so there is no edge or boundary to the universe. The universe is self-aware. It expands, bends, and continually recreates itself. The universe is constantly changing.

Being that you exist in a universe right now, knowing it is in a grand shift and spiraling through an alternate universe, imagine, with your eyes closed, that you are spiraling through every person on the planet Earth right now, rapidly, very, very rapidly. Imagine yourself spiraling through all those people — everyone.

You *are* a universe, as is everyone else. So let yourself spiral through every person on the planet at this precise moment. Focus on this carefully because this is very important. Be as quiet as you can be and focus as intensely as you can. There is a reason for doing it this way, and I will tell you what it is in just a moment.

As you are in the experience of spiraling through every person on the planet, you are exchanging atoms with them. This is simply letting you become a part of every person on the planet. You are becoming a part of every person on the planet, and you are letting every person on the planet become a part of you. As you are in the experience of becoming every person by having and letting every person become a part of you, let it go. Be done with it. You *are* that experience. You *are* the experience of your universe. You *are* the experience of your reality.

If this grand shift is to complete itself in 2013, which it most definitely will, you want to be ready for the completion of this shift so you can take yourself to the next experience of what you truly are.

The next step has to do with being a spirit, being a bit more nonphysical, having a thought process that functions at light speed rather than very slowly. With a higher functioning thought process, you will become very clear in your thinking. You will allow yourself to deal with situations of any nature in a very, very, very comfortable, loving, and gentle way. This all depends upon you and if you want to let it be that way, and I would assume you would want to allow it to be that way. It will be a choice, an individual choice. How would you like things to be? How would *you* like to be? Do you want to change and be more of who you truly are?

Become Your Own Reality

Now it is time to do one more thing. It is time to become your reality. You have let your reality become the universe. Now you are to let yourself become your reality. Begin thinking of your home, your automobile, your friends, your pets—begin thinking of everything in your reality. Begin thinking of everything and everyone in your reality with no judgment at all. Don't feel anything. All you are to do right now is think of all that without judgment. Don't react. Don't act. Don't do anything. Just think of all of it.

When I say, "Now," let all of that go away as quickly as you can. Let it all fade away.

"NOW."

Do it now, so you are left with only you as your reality. Begin replacing everything back into your reality, or what you call your reality. Replace everything. Put everything back in its place, but in a slightly different way—just a slightly different way. When you replace everything in your reality, when you put everything back in its place in your reality, imagine that everything and everyone is shining. Everything and everyone is shining. There is a glow of energy. There is an aura around everything and everyone, and you are seeing this aura around everything and everyone as you put everything and everyone back in its and their place in your reality. What you are doing is putting everything and everyone back inside of you.

You are doing this because you created all of it to begin with. So what you have just done with this exercise, is you have rearranged your entire being. You have restructured your entire being. What you have become is energy, your universe, everyone on the planet, your reality, all the things, situations, and people in your reality. You have *become* it all. You have become all of it. This is what you are. You are all of it.

This is why the shift is taking place—so you, and everyone else, can realize to a much greater extent that you are all of it. You are ALL of everything. *You are all of everything.*

With your eyes open, it might be a good thing for you to take a nice deep breath, refresh yourself, bring yourself back to your physical reality, and take a look around you. Look around you. Do you notice anything different about your reality? I think you might. If you don't, use this exercise a few more times, then you will have a most definite change. If you see things in a slightly different way, leave them alone. Let them be that way. They are functioning for you. They are doing what they know how to do for you. They are all serving you.

When You Act It Out, You Create It

Everything serves you all the time. Everything and everyone will always serve you. Why? Because you create it all. You create everything. You are all the creativity of what you would like to do. Everyone would like to do something very special and highly creative with his or her life. So what can it be? Ask yourself and tell yourself. You know what you would like to do. You know what it can be and what you would like to do. So once you tell yourself what you would like to do, understand and realize that you are already the energy of that. All you have to do is act it out. That is all you have to do. Act it out. When you act it out, you create it to be that way.

Let me say it again. *When you act it out, it will be that way. It becomes that.*

You have talents beyond your recognition. You have talents more than what you think you do; more talents than you think you have. May I suggest to you to simply try things, just try them, and when you are trying them, do not *TRY* them. Simply try them, and let them be fun as you are trying them. As you are trying them and letting them be fun while you are trying them, you will find more things you can do creatively.

If you are lazy, if you are depressed, if you are stuck or wallowing in misery, try doing something creative. Just try to have fun. Within minutes, you might find a new hidden talent you didn't know you had. Besides, if you are letting it be fun and you are having fun, how can you be depressed, miserable, or lazy? You cannot. When you are having fun and trying things out and experimenting, you are not making excuses about why you are not doing what you should be doing.

> **You are a part of God. You have the power to set anything right, to change anything.**

Remember one thing—you are creative energy, which is really saying you *are* everything, because God, or Infinite Intelligence, or whatever you name the life force, it is a creative energy. Everything is a creative energy, and everything is a part of God. You are a part of God.

Again, this has nothing to do with religion. If you are a part of God or All That Is, from this point on, it might be a bit hard to play the victim role when something does not go your way in your life. Remind yourself that you are a part of God, and you, yes you, do have the power, no matter what anyone or any religion tells you. Yes, you do have the power. You have the power to set anything right, to change *anything*.

Close your eyes and take one very deep, slow breath, inhaling through your nose. As you inhale, bring into your lungs and body an energy that is all about nature. Think about nature.

Do it now. Inhale slowly and deeply. Bring nature into your lungs. Let it fill your body. Hold your breath. Now gently open your mouth and gently blow out your breath.

Listen closely. Believe it or not, what you have just done is brought into your body the atoms of nature, the energy of nature. So, you have just become nature. Things are so very simple when you let them be that way.

I might suggest letting everything be simple, even yourself. Be simple.

Please don't misunderstand what I am saying. I am not telling you to be ignorant or a simpleton. No. I am saying to do everything in a very simple and uncomplicated way — in a very easy, gentle, simple way — because simplicity works best.

Love yourself more than you think you can.

Chapter 3

LETTING YOUR LIFE SHINE

L etting your life shine. Take a look at your life and your lifestyle as they are at this point. As you are looking at your life, how are things? How are they functioning? Are they functioning? Are things good? Are things very good? Are things just mediocre, or are things not so very good?

Also, look at yourself at this point in your life. How are you? Are you being creative? Are you being not so very creative? Do you feel stuck in the mud, or are you being brilliant?

Looking at, and thinking about, your lifestyle, is it really the way you want it to be? Is there room for improvement, or is it just what you have always wanted? If your lifestyle is just what you have always wanted, if your life is functional and functioning brilliantly, and if you are as creative as you can imagine yourself to be, then keep things as they are. If, on the other hand, your lifestyle is not quite the way you want it to be yet, you *can* have it the way you want it to be. If your life is not optimally functional, it can be more functional. You can learn how to have it be that way. If you think, or believe, you *can* be a bit more creative, today you will discover ways to become more creative.

> **Every thought you have will change your reality just a bit more.**

Every bit of creativity will lead to a vast pool of creative energy, because every time you are being creative, every time you are taking a creative action, everything you do in any creative way, brings you closer, and closer, and more into that vast pool of creative energy. To change your entire life, all you really need to do is slightly change your thinking—slightly—and this is all it will take.

The same will apply for being creative. Be slightly more creative in what you do. Every time you allow yourself to be that way, you will have more access to that pool of creative energy. This is what you want. When you exist in that vast pool of creative energy, you will never run out of ideas. You will always have inspiration. You will always have aliveness, and you will always know precisely what to do.

If you think at times you really don't know what to do or how to do it, simply stop what you are trying to do, take a couple of deep refreshing breaths, and think of what you would like to do, and see yourself doing it. Do not force the issue, but see yourself doing it in a very easy and gentle way, and something will begin to take place within your outer reality. A slight change will begin to take place. Every thought you have will change your reality just a bit more. Let me say it again. *Every thought you have will change your reality just a bit more.*

This is what you want. Bit by bit, by bit, by bit, because, too many times, when you try to have it all right now, you will find it does not happen. People have taught themselves to expect instant gratification, and sometimes you forget, or you are not aware, that certain steps need to be taken. Certain situations need to be developed "in order," so you can eventually have what you want. Eventually can be one day, it can be one week, or ten years. This will be up to you. Every thought you have will change your reality just a bit more.

Now, assuming you are being creative, maybe things are not creating themselves in the ways you want them to. Why? Why would this be? For example, you have an idea. You begin taking action with the idea, but, too many times, you view the outcome before you begin taking the necessary steps to create your idea as a reality.

Let me repeat this because this is really important. *Too many times, you view the outcome before you begin taking the necessary steps to create your idea as a reality.*

Stop what you are doing, take a deep breath, refresh yourself again, and think of your idea. When you think of your idea without looking at, or considering the outcome, you will begin to get more ideas about what you can do to take the necessary steps to create what you want.

When you think of your idea without looking at, or considering the outcome, you will begin to get more ideas about what you can do to take the necessary steps to create what you want.

45

Keep Things Simple

Thinking of your life, is there room for improvement? Think of your life, as it is right now, in a simple way. Do not complicate the issue. Think about your life in a simple way. If you were to break your life down to its most simple form, it would be one thing and one thing only, and that is an idea. It would only be an idea, because everything is an idea — everything. *Nothing is real until you make it that way.*

Begin with the idea of your life. It is simply an idea. Think of yourself floating out in space being your own universe as an energy form. You are going back to having your life be an idea before you were born, having a want, a desire, or a need for a life in physical form. It is an idea. It will present itself to you as an idea. Consider how you would like to create the idea of your life. How would you like your life to be in its most simple form? See it as an idea that will expand and grow within the structure of your own being, your own universe, because you are your universe.

When you are considering that in a very simple way, things will begin to come to you. Situations will come to you, and you will see them and you will feel them. Do nothing with them at this point. Not yet. Do nothing. Don't do anything. If you are seeing or feeling situations, or ways that your life *can* be, do nothing with them now. Just see them and/or feel them. Let them be. Let them be, because as long as you let them be, they will begin working for you.

If you begin by pushing things around, shoving things into place, nothing will work for you except anxiety and frustration, and you don't want this, especially as you are at the beginning point of creating your entire life from it being a very, very simple idea.

Thinking of how you would like your life to be, as things are coming to you, as ideas are coming to you, as situations are coming to you, as visions are coming to you, as possibilities are coming to you — begin letting all of them take their place. Everything will have its place in life and in your reality. Everything will have its own place. Begin allowing everything to take its place. If it seems as though something isn't working, let it do what it wants to do. If it is not working the way you think it should be working, it will reconstruct itself and begin to work for you if you can leave it alone and let it do its job. It knows what to do, because it is its own consciousness. It is its own reality, its own universe, and yes, it does indeed have its own emotional structure. *Everything* has an emotional structure. As you are leaving everything alone, as you are seeing and feeling everything, leaving everything alone, letting everything take its place, you might begin to notice a foundation. Upon this foundation, your life and your reality will be built.

Thinking of reality at this point, doing what you are doing with the idea of your life, begin considering reality as being something that will always change, and it will always change for one reason only, and that is to serve you, to bring you, and to give you everything you want. Reality is to give you everything you want. Think this to yourself, *"Reality is to give me everything I want."*

You have a universe that functions in the most optimal and complete way. It functions that way for YOU. There is an over abundance of everything in the universe, and the universe is just waiting, waiting, waiting to give it ALL to you. However, in order for you to allow it to give it all to you, you must do your part and take it. *Receive it.* Allow the universe to give it all to you, and allow yourself to receive it.

> **There is an over abundance of everything in the universe, and the universe is just waiting, waiting, waiting to give it ALL to you.**

Now is the time to look at your structure of emotionality. What do you believe about yourself? Do you believe that everything is within your reach, or do you believe that certain things, some things, or everything, is out of your reach? Do you believe you can allow the universe to give you everything you want, and do you give yourself permission to have everything? Begin with your emotion. How do you usually function emotionally? Do you function with a lot with anger, judgment, or fear? Begin to eliminate those emotions from your being. Judgment is a situation more than an emotion. Fear and anger are emotions, and you always have a choice as to which emotions you want to function.

There are, as "they" say, positive and negative emotions. Are there really positive and negative emotions? No, not really. Emotions are just emotions. Emotions are energy, and it is the judgment you place upon them that identifies and charges them. Ultimately, every emotion is a judgment in its own self. You can, if you want to, begin to train your emotions. Train them to function freely, no matter what they are—confusion, anger, depression, love, joy, happiness—all of them. Let them function completely, because when you do, you will find that negative emotions will no longer be negative, because they are having the opportunity to express themselves completely, which is what they always want to do. You will also find that all of your positive emotions are becoming a bit more creative, more constructive, and more positive in their own right, because you are also allowing them to express themselves completely.

Things Change

You have heard the words; things change. Things change. Now, close your eyes and in your mind, whisper to yourself, "things change" in a very gentle way. Do it again. "Things change." Whisper in a very gentle way: "Things change." If you do this a number of times, you will not fear change. The more you express anything, the more you will come to understand it. Once you understand something, then you can either let it go or use it to create your reality. Things change.

Now, close your eyes and say it a bit more loudly in your mind, a bit more happily. "Things change." "Things change." This is a good thing. Things do change. Change is a good thing, because change will allow you the opportunity to express yourself in more ways than you have been.

Expressing yourself will draw you out of your comfort zone, which is where people like to keep themselves. Many people keep themselves in emotional pain, because they know it and they are familiar with it, and it may seem to be more painful to change. Some people have become masters at self-sabotage and stay in that pattern because it is easier to function that way instead of making changes — changes that would ultimately take time, patience, and work.

There might be times when a comfort zone just might be a good thing. It *might* be. Usually, it creates itself as a prison, because when you are in a comfort zone, you are not willing to stretch yourself beyond the foundation and limitation of your comfort zone. That is what your comfort zone is — a grand limitation. Your comfort zone, when you really look at it, is mostly filled with fear and anxiety. You have become used to the feelings of fear and anxiety, because they have proven themselves workable, so you may not recognize them as fear and anxiety. You know they always work for you.

You can always have fear when you want. You can always have anxiety when you want. This is also a choice. You are not stuck with fear. You are not stuck with anxiety, nor are you stuck with love, joy, happiness, or anything else. Everything is a choice, and your life is a choice also. Your reality is a choice. You know this by now.

Find yourself having the idea of your life and letting things come to you, allowing and letting all those things take their place, letting all those things begin creating a new reality for you, and a new life for you. This isn't a hard thing to do. This is not a challenging thing for you. It will not make you lose what you have. It will not change you in any way other than to allow you to become more expressive and more creative.

By letting everything take its place, letting everything begin creating a new reality, a new life for you, you might find something taking place within you emotionally, maybe a slight sense of freedom. This is what you want, if you so choose. When you begin feeling freedom, do nothing with it at all. Simply let it reside within you, because it knows what to do. It knows what to bring you and when to bring it to you. Leave it alone as you have been leaving everything else alone to this point. Let it work for you. Let your life work for you. Let the idea of your life work for you. Let it create itself, and let freedom create itself in the best way for you. The more you let it, the more it will do just that for you.

> **You are your own grand opportunity.**
> **You are the grand opportunity of your life.**

As you begin feeling the freedom, as you are letting it be, you might just find something else taking place; a slight sense of opportunity. When and if you feel this — and again this is your choice — you can choose to feel it or not, but if you do, realize that opportunity is really what will take you from one step to the next step during the journey of your lifetime. You might know this by now, but how many times do you take the opportunity and do something with it? You are faced with, and presented with, opportunities all day long. The universe is the grandest opportunity there is. You are your own universe. You are your own grand opportunity. What does this mean to you?

This simply means that you have the chance, when you want to take it, to really do anything you want to do, in any way you want to do it, at any time you want to do it. When I say *chance*, I am not referring to something that might go wrong. "Well, I don't want to take the chance in doing that. It might blow up in my face." No, not at all. The structure and definition of chance is the opportunity to do or achieve something. Let chance also encompass change, because everything will change. All things change. Let the identity of chance change for you, and have it become another opportunity. So, you will have an opportunity within an opportunity. The opportunity is you. *You will have an opportunity to be in the opportunity of what you can be.*

Begin thinking that you are an opportunity, and that *you* are the opportunity — you are the *grand* opportunity of your life. When you begin thinking that way, you might find something else taking place within you; a bit more of an understanding of what you are really all about. This is what you want — just a bit. *Not too much at one time, just a bit, because when you have just a bit, you are apt to more easily let things reside within you.*

When you have it all, or a lot at one time, then you may feel bogged down. You may be in a hurry to force and push things into place so they can all work right. In time, they will not work at all, because you are forcing and pushing them. At this point, simply think how you feel about being completely in control of everything in your lifetime. See yourself, in your mind, being completely in control. You are controlling everything in your lifetime. You are in control of everything. Are things really working for you, or are they getting out of control?

Let Go of Control

When you try to control things, they may get out of control. Why? Because everything is consciousness. *Everything has consciousness. Everything is an idea.* Every idea will have its own emotional structure. When someone tries to force you to do something, do you enjoy it? Do you do it? Do you think, "No, I don't like the feeling. I won't do it. I'll do it my way, because I know what is best for me!" This is what everything else will do when you try to *control* it, when you try to force it onto place. It will fight you back. You may block the very thing you desire by trying to force it.

Leave things alone, if you want to. You don't have to, but it would serve you better if you did. It is your choice. If you want things to grow, if you want your life to expand and your reality to be what it really should be and can be, then leave things alone. Leave things alone, because everything knows what to do. Things, situations, ideas, really don't need your assistance or your control. They know what to do. How can this be? *Because you have created everything.* You will create all of your ideas. You. You will create your ideas for yourself.

By this time, you should be thinking a bit more clearly about what you are really all about and how you function. If you feel a sense of relief or freedom, then we will press on. If you feel frustration or anxiety, we will press on anyway.

So here we go. Looking at your lifestyle, how is your lifestyle? Is it, and I may have asked you this before, so here we go again—is it really just as you want it to be or is there room for improvement, or is it shut down? How is your lifestyle? If there is room for improvement, see how your lifestyle is. See what it is all about right now. What is it all about? Is it all about poverty? Riches? What? Creative energy? Being creative? Being lazy? How is your lifestyle? What is your lifestyle all about? Your lifestyle is what *you* are all about. YOU are your lifestyle. You create your lifestyle by, and with, what you do, how you do it, what you don't do, and how you don't do it. Your lifestyle is *what* you are. Your lifestyle is *how* you are. Your lifestyle is *why* you are right now. It seems that in a strange way, everything comes back to you. Everything you create, everything you can imagine, comes back to you. Why? Because it all begins within you.

> **You create your lifestyle by, and with, what you do, how you do it, what you don't do, and how you don't do it.**

In the first chapter, we talked about breaking through limitations. Everything is a limitation. Everything has a limitation until you begin slightly, slightly changing the foundation of your reality, your life, yourself, and your lifestyle. To *slightly* change everything, and to *greatly* change everything, all you need to do is slightly change the way you think about yourself. Put aside all the garbage you think about in your day, which is heaved onto you not only by yourself, but also by everyone and everything else. Give up thinking of that and everyone else's problems that they heave upon you for no reason at all, and just let all of that go. When you can, and if you can, give up what you have learned, because it is really not serving you. It might be serving you to a slight degree, but it really isn't. You want to break out of your comfort zone, and the way to do that is to let go of all the garbage. Let go of all the baggage, all the influence, and all the ways you have been taught. It is a very simple, easy, and quick thing to do, right?

Of course it is. All you have to do is make the choice and do it. "I choose to let go of everything, because I am worth more than all that baggage and all that garbage." That is all you need to do. If you say those words, feel the energy of those words. They will bring you into your state of freedom. Creative freedom.

> **Every thought you have about yourself will change your reality, because your reality is only an extension of you.**

How many ways can you be thinking of yourself? How many new ways? If you can't think of any new ways how about different ways? How many new or different ways can you begin thinking about yourself? Begin letting ways come to you. Allow them to come to you. The universe is working properly in a very good way. Your reality is being created in a very good way, because you are letting the ideas work. You are letting the ideas work, letting them take their place, and letting them do what they know how to do in the best way for you. How many new and different ways—even in slight ways, very slight ways—how many new and different, or different and new, slight ways, can you think about yourself?

Rather than thinking how you *have* been, think about how you *can* be. Really, how *can* you be? When you consider how you can be, you know you deserve it. You know you are worth it. You know there is no fear. You know there is no anxiety. You are only thinking of how you can be. You probably haven't really been creating how you can be, so you can't have fear or anxiety. Not yet. You might though, when you begin, and we will talk about that.

So, thinking of at least three or seventy-five thousand new ways you can slightly think about yourself, the choice is yours, because if you can think of three, you can think of, well really, one hundred seventy-five million ways. As you are thinking of new ways to think about yourself, something is taking place within the structure of your reality, because every thought you have about yourself will change your reality slightly. Every thought you have about yourself will change your reality, because your reality is only an extension of you. Your reality is an illusion. You direct your reality, but at the same time, you know it has its own consciousness. What you do is, you allow your reality to work for you. If you have an idea, this is a good thing. Take the idea. It is your idea and you are the creator of the idea, no matter what it might be.

A good idea or a bad idea. Many times, bad ideas become good ideas when you look at them in a different way. They are all equal. Everything is equal. Remember? Everything is energy.

Now you are thinking of one new way to think about yourself. Something is taking place within the structure of your reality. It is thinking about itself in the same, but slightly new way—a slightly new way, but just that slight bit of a new way will allow your entire reality to change completely. There are no big ideas or small ideas. There are no big thoughts or small thoughts. All thoughts are energy, and everything is equal. There are *just*, and *only*, ideas. There are *just*, and *only*, thoughts. When I say to slightly think about yourself in a new way, I am tricking you. To think of your self in a slight way is to think of yourself in a grand way. Are you catching on? Of course you are.

As you think about yourself in a different way, you feel a bit more freedom within the structure of your reality, which will allow you to express yourself in a complete way, so you can be more creative the next time you have an idea. All this adds up to what? All of it adds up to being the way you really can be. Should you be a certain way? If you want to you can, but "should" is tricky word. Maybe you "SHOULD" not anything, but maybe you "CAN" everything—if and when you want to.

You have an idea. You begin doing something with the idea. You know you are worth it. You know you are worthy. You deserve it. You deserve everything. You know all of this by now. As you are creating something with the idea, you will have limitations pop up—fear, anxiety, and all the rest. You may think you do not really deserve it after all, and you will go over all of your limitations, one at a time, or all at once. That will be up to you. That is your choice also.

> **You are the master creator of your entire life, your entire lifestyle, and your universe.**

How do you like to look at your limitations—all at one time, or one at a time? How about not even looking at them at all? If you do have limitations, so what? Don't look at them or acknowledge them. Don't focus on them, because when you do, they will magically appear and prevent you from doing something, because you are feeding them energy.

You are giving them energy. You are focused upon them. Even if you do have limitations, which really you don't—but yes, you do, because you believe you do—don't even think of them, and simply take the idea and see how you would like to cause the idea to become a reality, and simply do it. Just simply do it. If you feel fear, anxiety, or anything else, know that all emotions are equal. There is only equality. Everything is equal. Fear might just be strength, vitality, or excitement. It all depends upon how you perceive it, how you judge it, how you accept it, and how you allow it.

You create your own reality.

You are the creator of your own complete reality. I think it would be a good thing to remind you of that. So hey, you are the master creator of your entire reality, your entire life, your entire lifestyle, and your universe. These words mean absolutely nothing until you let them have meaning. All of these words, *you create your own reality*, those words—what power can you give them? How can you define them? You create your own reality. You create your own reality.

These are just words, and words are just sounds put together to sound like words. How to *charge* them is to say them repeatedly, "I am the creator of my own reality, I am the creator of my own reality." Say it over and over again and within a few seconds time, you will begin to feel the power of those words. You will begin to feel the words within you.

This is what you want, because the words themselves mean nothing. The power of the words means everything, and that power can take you out of your comfort zone in such an easy and gentle way. So easy and gentle, that you won't even know you are breaking free of your own prison. Therefore, you will have no fear of stepping out of your boundary. Then, at that point, you are free to do anything you want, in any absolute way you want, because you are the absolute of your own life. You are the absolute of your own entire life. You are the absolute of your life. That means, you are it, kid! You are everything. *You are the All That Is, and within the All That Is.* You have all the power imaginable to create anything—in any way you would like it to be.

Your life, your lifestyle, your reality, is all up to you. What a freedom. What a joy. If you are the absolute of your own life, then you are the absolute of everything. If you are the absolute of everything, everything is the absolute within you, of you, and with you. Your life, right now, is absolute, whether it is just the way you want it or not. If it is, let it continue. If it is not, appreciate it. Appreciate it and it will be everything you want. I am saying to you— *appreciation will change the structure of everything very quickly.* When you appreciate what you have, you are not focused on what you don't have. What you don't have will mean nothing to you. It means nothing. Then what do you have? When you appreciate what you have, then you have the freedom to do anything you want in any way you want.

You exist in that vast pool of creative energy all the time. You exist in that. You have become that. You have created that. There was no beginning and there can be no ending. It always has been and it always will be, and it is right now. Pull everything you want into your "now moment" in time. Have a plan. Having a plan is a very good thing, but know that your plan will always change, *so be prepared to agree with the change*. Once you put your plan into effect, then you let it create itself for you, and it will. As it is creating itself, if it sees something that might not be that good for you, it will change its structure. This is why your plans change.

If you are a hardhead, and if you just continue along the same path, you may have a problem. If you are easy-going, knowing and having faith in what you are doing, and if you agree with the change, then you will have won the game. Everything will be perfection, because everything *is* perfection right now. Do you understand that? Everything is in perfection right now because what you have, you created. You created in perfection. *The universe has manifested for you, your thoughts, desires, and beliefs.* You need only to see it in that way. You need only to see it in that way, if you want to. This is your choice also.

Your life, your lifestyle, your reality are all about you, kid! It is all about you. It is all about you. This should empower you to the nth degree. Everything is all about you. It is ALL about you. You have the say-so. You have the say-so over everything. Yes, you do. You do. You alone do.

When I say that it is all about you, I am speaking to every aspect of you, everything about you. I am speaking to the complete and absolute, you.

> **You are the absolute of your life.**
> **That means, you are it, kid!**
> **You are everything.**

When something is said to you, don't try to break down what you are so you can fit what is said to you into a certain category of your being-ness. Begin looking at yourself. Begin thinking of yourself as being the absolute, the everything—not this level, that level, the conscious, the unconscious or the super-conscious. Be very simple and simplify your thinking. You are ONE being. This is what you are, one idea. You are one idea. Keep yourself that way. Things will be easier for you.

Listen very carefully to what I am about to say. Your ego is not your enemy. The ego has been grossly misunderstood. What your ego is—and please pay attention to this—what your ego is, is your daily point of motivation. That is all it is. This is all it can be. That is its function. Thinking that way, your ego can never lead you astray. It can only, and always, point you in the right direction, because it is only your daily, or momentary, point of motivation. When things seem to lead you astray, or into different areas, maybe you are doing that for a reason, and the reason is to discover a bit more about how you can take the same idea and do something else with the idea. Change the structure of the idea.

> **Your ego is not your enemy. What your ego is, is your daily point of motivation. That's all it is.**

Why would you create cancer if you enjoy smoking cigarettes? Why not create a cancer-free body, which is what you are. The natural state of the body is health—a disease free organism. This is what you are. Why would you create illness? Something you need exists in that illness. *Something you need exists in that illness.* Find out what it might be. You can create anything you want, whether it is cancer, or love, or joy, or death, or anything. You can create anything you want. Think about how you would like to create. Understand that your beliefs, thoughts, and emotions create your reality. It is all your own choice. Do not complicate your thinking. Think in a very simple way, and before you do anything, always give yourself permission to have everything.

As a physical human being, you cannot exist without negative energy or negative emotions. You cannot do it, and why can't you? Because you label emotions and put judgments on them. Human beings are really good at that. What you can do is allow the negative energy and/or emotion to serve you. So how would it serve you? For example, if you have fear, how can fear serve you? It can very simply point you in a different direction—lead you away from what you are about to do, which might or might not be a good thing for you. This is how fear can serve you.

Give yourself permission to have everything, one thing at a time. If there is something you want, give yourself permission to have just that one thing you want. Then you won't have to take on all the negatives. Do you want what you are thinking of? Yes, or no? Be simple. Yes, or no? Do you give yourself permission to have it? Yes, or no? Be simple. Do you really believe you deserve it? Simply, yes or no? Do you believe you can have it? Simply, yes or no? Then you have no problem.

Focus on it, and you can have it and let it work for you. Do not force it. Let it work for you, but focus upon it at the same time. *See yourself as having it right now.*

You have your talent, you have it all now, and everything is now. What is the catch? You believe in time. Time is man-made and it is only another illusion. This is why you say, "Well, I haven't achieved it yet. I'll achieve it in five years." You say things like this only because of your belief in time. You have everything within your reach, within your being, right now. Of course you do. This is the way it is, and all you need to do to achieve the level of success that you want, is to begin expressing what you do. *Express it.* This is all you need to do, and you will be on your way. Are you willing to try it? Believe that you are brilliant, and be that way every chance you have.

Chapter 4

TAKING IT TO
THE NEXT LEVEL

When I ask you how you are feeling, what is the first thing that comes to your mind? Do you first think of your feeling, or do you just allow it to be within you and express it? How are you feeling?

As you are going throughout your day, when you are doing things in your day, do you think about what you are doing or do you just do things without thinking and without analyzing? When you are thinking of what you are doing, what are you really thinking about? When you think about it, you are really not thinking about what you are doing, because you are thinking about something else. Your mind wanders. When you *are* thinking about what you are doing, what are you thinking about? The outcome? What you are going to get out of it? Is someone going to like it?

Let's go with, *what you are going to get out of it.* There is a flip side to this coin, because many times, when you think about what you are going to get, you also think about what comes with what you are going to get. That can be the fun part of it, but there can be a miserable part too. It all depends on how you are thinking about what you are doing. You know by now that you are creative. You are of a creative source, force, or energy, and you have a plan for your life. Now, thinking about your life plan at this point, how is it coming along? How are you doing with executing your plan? Are you feeling joy in your life? Are you learning what joy is? Joy is good for you, because when you can be realized within joy, and when you think about what you are doing, you will actually be thinking about what you *can do* with what you are doing.

Think about this. Let's assume you are doing something. We will just imagine right now. So, you are doing something and you are thinking about what you are doing, but all the side thoughts you are having have nothing to do with what you are doing. They will be about what might go right, what might go wrong, what else you can do, what you will be doing tomorrow, what you will have for dinner, how your lunch was, and everything else. When you think about what you are doing, being in joy, you will be able to think about everything else that will come along your way when you think about what you can have, or get from, what you are doing. Everything you do will bring you something in your lifetime. No matter what you do, everything you do will bring you something. That something will always have two sides or opposing forces to it, or in it, or within it. If you are in joy, if you are of joy, in the experience of joy—if you have joy within you, then you can focus on everything good and positive that will come your way.

> **Joy is nothing more than understanding what you are feeling, what you are doing, and what you are all about. When you can understand what you are all about, you are joy.**

Realize, I am not telling you to always be of joy. That is ridiculous and nearly impossible, because most of the time, the last thing you are thinking about is joy. You won't be of joy or in joy, when you are not feeling or having joy. You may be depressed, grieving, pissed off, discouraged, and all the rest. That is okay and a good thing, because you must experience all your emotions all the time. Now, when you are in the experience of emotions that are not of joy, simply find the joy in the emotion that you are experiencing. It is as hard or easy as you make it. Everything has joy. *Joy is nothing more than understanding what you are feeling, understanding what you are doing, and understanding what you are all about.* When you can understand what you are all about, you are joy. When you can understand what you are doing, you are doing it with, out of, and in joy.

You go through your day. You do things. You think about what you are doing, but you are really not thinking about what you are doing. You are thinking about what you can get from what you are doing, or how you hate what you are doing. You are also thinking about all the things that will come with what you will get. Looking at your present self, how different are you from the way you used to be?

Understand and realize that you will change every day. You change every day. You are a new individual every day. You wake up from sleep being a new person, a new energy, a new creative force, every day. You are also not now, at this moment, the same person you were an hour ago. So tell me, how are you different now than the way you used to be?

If you think you are not so very different now, or today, than the way you used to be, then you have some inner work to do. You can begin to look within yourself and take a long hard look at how you used to be. When you begin thinking of how you used to be, you would also begin thinking of how you used to do things, what you used to expect, what came to you from the things you used to do. You will also think of all the side issues, side situations, side thoughts, side feelings, and side emotions that will be attached to how you are thinking about what you used to do and how you used to do what you used to do.

When you can think of all that, and really place yourself in more of the present and become a bit different—different from the way you used to be—simply let go of how you think you should be. Too many times, people think they should be a certain way thinking that they should do this in this way, should do that in that way. Thinking like that only causes you to remain as you used to be. Shoulds are really not a very good idea. You should really nothing. You *can* everything. To change and to change your life, begin thinking of everything that *can* be, how it CAN be, when it CAN be, and why it CAN be.

Also, look at yourself right now. If you are very different or just somewhat different from the way you used to be, then what have you been thinking about? Maybe you have been thinking about letting yourself be free within your creative structure or creative energy. To allow yourself to be free in your creative structure or creative energy is to allow yourself, and to let yourself, be free within the joy of understanding who you are, what you are, and why you are.

How many times have you thought, "Well, who am I, what am I, and why am I?" If you haven't thought of that lately, think about it now. Who are you? What are you, and why are you? You know who you are, or you think you do, and you most certainly know what you are, or you think you do, but why are you? Setting aside who you are, what you are—why are you? *Why are you in this lifetime?*

The answer is simple and uncomplicated. *You are here to create.* Again, you are here to create. No matter what it is, you are to create, and you have your ideas of what you would like to create. Let me ask you this, on a scale from zero to one hundred percent, how creative are you lately? Be honest with yourself. How creative are you lately?

> **You really should nothing. You can everything. To change your life, begin thinking of everything that *can* be, how it *can* be, when it *can* be, and why it *can* be.**

Now is the time to take yourself to your next level. Thinking of your next level, what do you think it *can* be? Keep it simple. What do you think will be your next level? Take yourself beyond what you are thinking, and really, and I mean REALLY, let the creative force within you fly free. Let go of all thought. Let go of your power to analyze. Let go of how you rationalize things in your life and just for the moment, be free-flying creativity. Let yourself be free-flying creativity and a force that has nothing in the way. A force that is free to do anything, to be anything. What do you think, or what can you see your next level as being? Quickly, and don't think about it.

Would it be totally confident? Feeling great? Merging? Making a difference? Understand and realize this is what you are NOW. I know what you are thinking, and you want to say, "I understand and realize that." If you do, then why aren't you being that way? Let me tell you why you are not. Because you are thinking of all the things that are attached to your thoughts that you have about what you are doing, and what you will get from what you are doing. What can you do with all of that? I will tell you. You can simply stop thinking the way you have *been* thinking and stop thinking the way you *are* thinking, and begin to change your thought pattern. Begin to change your thought pattern. Begin changing how you think about yourself and your reality. Let me ask you. If you had one opportunity right now to have your reality be any way you would like it to be, how would it be?

Change Your Thought Pattern

Gently close your eyes and gently take a deep breath. Inhale through your nose. Exhale through your nose, and begin to relax your body. Relax your body. Relax. Take another deep breath. Inhale through your nose. Exhale through your nose, and let your body relax a bit more. Focus on your spirit, the force within you that is all about creativity and creative energy. You might want to let yourself feel your force. Feel the energy within you. Be in the experience of your own creative force. Be in the experience of your own creative force. Feel your own energy. Let go of your physical body and feel your energy. Simply feel your energy.

As you are feeling your energy, take one deep breath. Inhale through your nose. Exhale through your mouth, gently. Relax yourself more, and be your larger energy. Be more of your own creative force right now. As you are doing this, mentally see your reality entering into a wide mouth of a funnel, coming into you through the narrow mouth of the funnel at the top of your head. Your reality is coming into you, into the force that you are, into your creative energy. Feel your reality coming into your creative force, into your energy, and as it does so, allow your reality to become nothing more than pure, creative energy.

Begin merging yourself with your reality. Blend your energy with that of your reality, and just let everything sit within you for a moment. Take a deep breath. Inhale through your nose. Exhale through your mouth and begin to see within you a

71

joy. I want you to see a joy. You can give it any form or any shape that you want to. See a joy within you. As you are seeing the joy, give it a color. Have it appear very soothing to you, and feel the energy of the joy. It doesn't have to be a very excited energy. It can be a very calm, relaxing energy. See a joy within you. Give it form. Give it shape. Give it mass. Give it an identity. Let it have an identity. Let it assume its own identity. Give it a reason to be within you right now. Give it a reason to be within you, and that reason might be to allow you to be more realized within yourself as being a joy. Be a joy.

Have that joy mix in with your creative force and the energy of your reality. Blend it. Have all the energies swirling within each other and intertwining within each other. As you are doing this, begin feeling what your next level might be or can be. Now, I might give you a small clue to what it might or can be. That is greatness. GREATNESS. Let this idea of greatness join with your creative force, your energy, the energy of your reality, and the joy. Have all that mix together, and feel the greatness blending with all the other energies. Greatness is an energy, but it is also the energy of what you are really all about. Have all of this blend and merge within you.

Take one deep breath. Inhale through your nose and exhale through your nose. Imagine you are replacing your reality as it was, but in a brand new way, by filling it with joy. See and feel it filled with joy, because you know the joy will bring you the freedom to be more creative—more than you ever have been in your life to this point. Replace your reality as it was, but this time it is filled with joy. Everything in your reality is filled with joy. This doesn't mean you have to smile all the time or you have to tell everyone that you love them. No. Joy is a force of creativity. It will allow you to expand, open up, and become far more creative.

As you become more creative, see yourself in your imagination, right now, being more creative, and creating what you have been thinking about for your life and for your reality. I want you to see yourself creating what you have been thinking about, what you have been wishing for, what you have been hoping for. See yourself creating it.

> **Self-love will give you the freedom to truly love and accept others for who, what, and why they are.**

As you are doing this, feel the result as you are seeing yourself creating what you have been thinking about. *Feel* the result. What is the result? The result is self-love. This is the result. Self-love. What you have been creating leads to self-love. Self-love is an abiding love and appreciation for, and acceptance of, the intimate connection with who you are, what you are, and why you are. Having self-love will give you the freedom to truly love and accept others for who, what, and why they are.

What you can do is take one deep breath. Inhale through your nose. Exhale through your nose, and if you would like to, feel self-love, not only inside of

73

you, but all around you. Feel it on your skin. Feel your skin tingling from the energy of self-love. When you can do this, expand the energy of your self-love and fill the room you are in, right now, and then fill your entire home, right now, and fill your entire reality, right now. Fill it again.

You are charging your reality with your love, which will simply allow your reality to work in a complete way for you, so you can complete everything you want to—so you can be a success—so you can simply be more creative when you want to be. So you can be more creative and more functional, without even thinking about what you are doing. So, take a nice deep breath with your eyes wide open. How do you feel?

Define the level you have just created. Take a look at this level you have just created. Take a look at it. Get to know it. Feel it. Realize it. Sense it. Get to know it in every way you can imagine. THIS IS WHY YOU ARE. This awareness that you just created is *why* you are. It is also *who* you are, and it is also *what* you are. Having created this next level, you understand more and realize more of what you are really all about.

Think about your identity. Within your identity, there is a duality. There are positives. There are negatives. There are goods. There are bads. There are rights and there are wrongs. Have all the goods, bads, rights, wrongs, positives, and negatives, merge and become a force, a simple force. Close your eyes and see all of them merging and becoming a force. See it in any way you would like to. Imagine all the goods, bads, rights, wrongs, positives, and negatives, merging to form a force, to create a force. See the force, and give it a shape. It has its own meaning. Give it a shape. See it in any way you would like to see it. What you are seeing is a representation of you. You are seeing yourself. You are that force. You are what used to be that duality. You have merged within yourself to create yourself as being a force.

Keeping your eyes closed, simply imagine that you are beginning, right now, to do something you have never done before in your lifetime. I don't care what it is. Imagine something. I won't tell you what to imagine. Imagine you are beginning to do something you have never done before in this lifetime. See yourself as this force doing this with grandness and greatness. Let yourself be grand and great in this moment. See yourself in a grand way doing something you have never done before in your life—it can be anything. See yourself doing it with grandness and greatness.

With your eyes closed gently, how you are feeling? Gently, with your eyes closed, how are you feeling? Now, open your eyes and be present.

Think of what you are doing right now. What are you doing right now? As you are thinking about what you are doing, what are you really thinking about? Are you thinking or are you feeling? Are you reacting, and if you are reacting, how are you reacting? If you had the opportunity, with nothing attached to it at all, if you had the opportunity, right now, to create yourself in a brand new way, what would that way be? If you had the opportunity to have your reality be any way you want it to be, or would like it to be, how would it be? Stress free? Money in the bank? Easy?

I am going to use the word "must" in a very positive way. You must understand, right now, this is the way your reality is, and you need to understand, right now, this is the way you are. You really are this way, because you really are your reality. You create your reality with your thoughts, with your emotions, and with your beliefs. Many times, you create it in ways that do not work for you in the best way. Many times, you *do* create your reality to work for you in the best way.

When you are creating your reality to work for you in the best way, what are you thinking about? Are you worried about someone else's expectations of you? Are you worried you won't be good enough? Are you worried people will change their opinion of you? When you are creating your reality to serve you, for you to be brilliant and to have no expectations of, or from your reality, and when you are creating your reality to work for you and to serve you for your highest good, you are not having expectations of your reality. You are letting your reality be what it is, and when you let it be what it is, it will work for you all the time.

Your reality is consciousness. It is an extension of you. It has emotions. It has feelings. It is energy. It is consciousness. It is an extension of you. If you can allow your reality to be what it is, it will work for you for your highest good.

That must mean—and again I use the word "must" in a positive way—that must mean if you can let yourself be, then you will create more and more of what you want, and you will be serving yourself for your highest good. Here comes the big question. Can you let yourself be?

By that I mean, can you simply be without judgment, without expectation in a negative sense, or of a positive sense? Can you just be without anything attached to you? Can you be without limitation? Can you be without anyone else's belief? Can you? Yes, or no? Do you think you can?

Would you like to *be*? If you can, and if you are, do you know what that means? Do you really know what that means? IT MEANS YOU ARE FREE.

If you are free, then you are not in judgment of anything or anyone. You are not thinking of limitation. You are not thinking about what you are doing. You are not thinking about what you will get from what you are doing. You are not thinking about what anyone else will think of you. You are not accepting anyone else's belief into your reality. You are NOT anything. What you ARE is pure creative energy—a force that has no beginning and no ending. A force that just continues to recreate itself in the grandest way it can imagine. Now, do you think you can be that? Yes, or no? Can you really be that?

You can decide that. So, make a choice. If you really would like to be that way—make the choice to be that way. Let me tell you something. If you choose to be that way, when something or someone pops into your reality that doesn't match your creative force or your energy, what can you do? When things take place in your reality that are not serving you for your highest good, do not fight them. Do not judge them. You will let them be what they are and step back from them. You will observe them and let them play themselves out, and then you will let them go. This is one more way to take yourself to the next level. With practice, you can do this.

Think of your reality, right now. Surely there are things, situations, ideas, and/or people in your reality that try you emotionally in a negative way. Having taken yourself to your next level and being your next level, your job now — which will be a job filled with joy — your joy job is to observe everything, acknowledge everything, let everything play itself out, and let everything go. Certainly, I am not telling you to simply sit, watch everything, let it go, and sit and grow old and die. I am not telling you to do that at all. When you can be the observer, then you really and truly are the creator. Observe, allow, let go and do what? Can you think of something else you can do?

Love Your Creation

Love your creation. No matter what it may be. Be your own sense of joy. Let everything go, and focus on yourself, and be the power that you are. You are a creative force. Are you beginning to know yourself as being that creative force? If you are, good for you. For the next week, I would like for you to take yourself to the next level again, by simply being that force of creative energy. That means having no judgments, having no limitations, having no excuses, and just allowing yourself to simply be creatively and completely free. It also means you will not think of what you are doing. You will not think of the result. You will not think of what you can get from what you are doing. You will not think about all the busy chatter that comes along with thinking about what you will get from what you are thinking about and what you are doing.

Your focus will only be on serving yourself for your highest good. This is not being egotistical. It is not being selfish. It is only re-centering yourself within yourself, and re-realizing yourself as being the power that you really are. This will be your job for the next week. Do you think you would like to do it?

What will you do when you find yourself being in judgment? What will you do? When you find yourself being in judgment, observe it, recognize it, acknowledge it, and let it fade away.

How are you feeling? Let me ask you something else. How old are you? How old are you feeling? Guess what. You are ageless. Since there is no time, how old you are means nothing. You are brand new with each moment, and people lose sight of that momentarily. You are thousands of years old by man's time, and have lived many, many lives. So what? You are brand new with every moment of time. You are learning, through many lives and experiences, to be of pure consciousness, and to exist as pure consciousness. When you exist as consciousness, you are really nowhere, but you are everywhere at the same time. You can create realities when you want or need to. You can create a reality to be just like this reality, if you want to. You can create nothingness, if you want to. How about thinking more of yourself as being that creative force?

If you can let go a bit more of the physical you, you will be able to create much more in your life and for your reality, and for yourself. Let me add one more thing. No matter what you do, no matter what you think of, no matter how you think, keep it simple. Keep it simple. Simple works.

People tend to get so caught up in drama and feeling sorry for themselves. What if you are at rock bottom? Maybe this is the best place you can be in your life. What would you really, and I mean *really*, like to do in your life? Realize you are at the best place you can be, because now you can do anything you want, with no restrictions at all. As an example, what if what you really want to do is write? What will you be writing about? Be specific. Let's say your answer is to write about love and relationships.

Right now, in this time, people are losing sight of their relationships, their love, and the love they have, or used to have. People are also losing sight of self-love. In your writing you can bring everyone's thoughts and feelings back to loving the self, which will allow them to love others, and to have more relationships with better and deeper meaning.

With whatever you have in mind for what you want to do, begin by making a commitment to yourself — today.

Okay, what time today will you make that commitment? What would you like your emotions to be? Feel the emotions now. When you feel it, you can do it. Stop being lazy, stuck, and coming up with excuses. Don't feel sorry for yourself and begin being the force that you really are.

Do you think you can do it? Of course you can do it.

Chapter 5

CHANNELING THE HIGHER SELF

C hanneling the higher self. There are a few ways to channel. Channeling means directing. The higher self is simply that part of you that is in touch with all aspects of the entire you—more aspects of what you really are, because, as you know, you are much more than what you appear to be. You are much more than what and how people see you to be. You are always, always more than how you think about yourself, and you are *always* much more than what you think you are.

There are aspects of you that are acting out their identity all the time throughout your day—throughout every day, throughout your week, your month, your year, and your entire lifetime. Ninety percent of those aspects are functioning, I will say, in different levels within your awareness—your consciousness, your unconsciousness, or subconsciousness. This means, as they function, they are acting out their roles during your life, and you don't even know it. You have no conscious awareness of what they are doing or how they are doing what they're doing, but the higher self is in touch with ALL the aspects of what you are really all about. There is a constant flow of communication.

Some people think, and they might say, that the higher self is the subconscious mind. No, not really. The subconscious mind is a part of the higher self, and the higher self is a part of the subconscious mind. The unconscious mind is a part of the higher self and vice versa. The conscious mind is also a part of the higher self. The higher self is also a part of the conscious mind. They all work together and you can't really separate them. They are all working together all the time with a constant flow of communication.

> **You are much more than what and how people see you to be.**

Think of the times when, consciously, you get a grand inspiration or brand new idea. This is the higher self within you bringing to your conscious mind a new thought, a new idea, or a new inspiration. Many times, the higher self deals with what you call the Hall of Records or the Akashic Records. Now, really, the Hall of Records and the Akashic Records are ideas that exist within you. All of those records that people think are floating out in space are really a part of you. To access the Akashic Records, what you need to do is direct your higher self, and open up your awareness within your higher self, so it can consciously bring to you all the information, or any of the information you need, either from the Hall of Records or the Akashic Records. Let me say that again. These places exist *within* you.

Channeling is directing. You direct energies in your life. You direct energies in your day. You direct energies in your body. When you feel out of sorts, maybe ill, maybe sick for a time, you direct healing energies in and around your body to heal your body. Many times, you direct energy around your body and those energies will stay with you, and in time they will blend with your body. Sometimes, you will direct energies in or out of your body.

One reason for directing energy out of your body would be to stimulate what you call your chakra points or access points of energy, or energy points. I'll call them energy points. When you direct energy outside of your body, the energy points become stimulated and they function to a higher degree and more completely. Your consciousness, your subconsciousness, your unconsciousness are all functioning completely all the time. The higher self, being a part of all of them, and all of them being a part of the higher self, is really more of what you are all about. The higher self has access to ALL aspects of your entire being. Your entirety.

Some of those aspects do exist in other dimensions of your present reality. Looking at your reality, you can recognize it, realize it, but understand your reality to be nothing more than energy — an illusion. As the foundation or the structure of your reality changes, your aspects will change also. The aspects of you — and all the personalities that exist that you don't know of, because you do not feel all of them — are functioning in their own right and changing within their own right. They are changing their foundation and their structure to match the dimensions they exist in and function within. Think that everything is in a state of change, which includes your higher self. It is always in a state of change.

On to directing the higher self, channeling the higher self, or directing the consciousness of the higher self. In a sense, even though it is a part of your conscious, subconscious, and unconscious, it has its own consciousness also. Within its consciousness will lie and will be found, those Akashic Records that exist within you. They are a part of you. They exist in what you call your higher self. There are ways to channel the higher self and all the information found in the higher self.

An Exercise to Access Your Higher Self

Close your eyes and take a deep breath. Begin to relax yourself and imagine that you are walking into a room. In this room is one chair, a big, fluffy, comfortable, warm chair. Sit in the chair. As you sit in the chair, you find yourself becoming more relaxed. As you are becoming more relaxed sitting in the chair, you will feel something becoming different around you and inside of you. Something is changing. If you can allow the change, you will feel this something as a sense of an opening within you to other dimensions of your present reality, and to some of the aspects of you that you are unaware of. Allow things to change.

Let this opening take place and simply become aware, if you can right now, become aware of some of the other aspects of you. Become aware of other dimensions of your present reality. Just be the observer. Just observe all of it for right now. Do nothing else. Only, and just, observe it all. Look it over. See what it has to offer you. See how it is functioning within its own right. See what is taking place in the dimensions, and see how the aspects of you are being functional in those dimensions. Just see it all. This is all you should be doing at this point. See it. Do nothing else. Have no reaction. Have no emotional response. Just see it.

Now, being in your chair, relaxing more, and allowing yourself to relax more and more, take another deep breath, and relax yourself even deeper. Think of something that you are working on, or working with, in your life. Think of something you are working on, or with, at this point in your life. Being relaxed, what you can now do is simply ask for your higher self to bring to you, the *aspect* of your complete self that will help you to understand and complete what you are working on, or with, at this point, at this time, in your life. You do not have to know what the higher self looks like. If you need to see it, give it a form. Give it a shape—any form, any shape you would like it to have. Go ahead and do it. That will be fine.

Ask it to bring to you the aspect of your complete self that will help you with what you are working on, or working with, at this point in your life. All you have to do is ask that aspect of you what you need to do. Then listen. Observe the aspect, because it will speak with you. It will guide you. It will tell you what you need to do, what you can do, and what you should do. Do this right now. Take a moment and ask that aspect of you what you need to do and let it tell you. You may hear it as words audibly or you may hear it within you. You may sense the answer, or you may feel the answer coming to you. Allow it to come to you in any way it wants to, and it will. Do it right now. Take a moment and do it. If you find you are having a hard time connecting with the aspect of you, it is all right. Let it go. Take a break, and you can repeat this exercise another time.

Once you have your answer, thank the aspect for its help and focus back within yourself. Focus back within yourself. Take a deep breath to refresh yourself. Open your eyes. If you are still sitting in the chair, good. If you are not, that is all right too, because you will be back in the chair again. Take note of how you feel. You may feel a bit different. You may feel complete and a bit larger in your energy. This is what happens when you connect and communicate with the aspects of you or your higher self. You are dealing with a much larger energy, because you are much larger than you allow yourself to be in your daily life and in your daily routine. You may feel larger or a bit dizzy, which is all right, because you will need to get used to the feeling of larger energy. This is normal.

What you can do now is close your eyes again. Simply be in that room again and look at the chair. Just look at the chair. If you are still sitting in it, get up and just look at the chair. Looking at the chair, ask it what it can do for you other than to relax you. Ask it what it can do for you and let it answer you. You may hear words. You may feel the answer inside of you. Let it answer you. Know what it is telling you. Recognize what it is telling you. Accept what it is telling you, because it can, and will, do a lot for you from this time on. If you want to, and if you would like to, you will, or you can, be using this chair for a long time in this lifetime, and we will explore other ways to use this chair as we go along. Ask it again now, what it can do for you and let it answer you. Do it right now.

Seeing yourself in the room, sit in the chair again. Sit in the chair. Take a deep breath. Refresh yourself, relax yourself, and let your relaxation become very deep. Feel good. Feel relaxed. Feel powerful and feel creative, because now you will begin to use more of your creative energy, and the chair will help you.

Sitting in the chair, relaxing more, feeling more powerful, feeling more creative, ask your higher self to bring to you one aspect of you that deals entirely in, and with, creative energy — the aspect of creating reality and being creative. When that aspect shows itself to you, or appears to you, you may see it in a number of different ways — a form, a person, an individual, a mass of energy, exploding energy, or twinkling energy. Because it is all about creation, it can appear to you in any way. You may see it as recreating itself with every moment of time, having a new form, a new shape. It may show itself as a complete and entire universe. It might be a star, a symbol, or a color. However it shows itself to you, accept it. Don't reject it. Ask it to help you use your creative energy in a complete way. Ask it that right now. It will agree. It can't not agree with you, because it is to serve you. It is to help you, because it is a part of you. What you are doing is bringing up, bringing out, and bringing forth, that creative part of you now.

Think again of the thing, the idea, the situation you are working on, or you are working with in your life, and ask that aspect of you if it will please help you to be more creative in manifesting, or completing what you are working on, or what you are working with. As it helps you, ask what else you need to do to complete what you are working on, or with, at this time in your life. What else would you need to do? Let it give you the answer. Hear words or feel the answer within you. Do it now. Now, thank that aspect of you. Know what that aspect told you.

Again, if you are having a hard time connecting, let it go for now. You can repeat this another time. You can practice this technique for the rest of your life with anything, any situation or idea that will come to you for the rest of your lifetime, or you can simply let it all go and go on as you have been going on. This will be up to you. If you want to use this technique, it will be a good thing, but you must realize one thing; no, before I tell you this, I will give you one more technique then I'll tell you the news.

You are standing in the room looking at the chair. I want you to ask the chair what you can do for it. Ask the chair what you can do for it, so it can provide you with more of what you want and need. Let it tell you what you can do for it. Ask it right now. In your mind, in your imagination, right now, see yourself doing exactly what it told you that you could do for it. See yourself doing it, doing that for the chair. Do it right now. Go ahead, take a moment, and do it right now. In your own way, I would like you to do one thing—and this might sound a bit odd. I would like you to make a pact or a bond with the chair. Talk to the chair and make a deal with the chair that as long as it serves you— you will serve it. Make that deal right now. Go ahead, take a moment, and do it.

Sit in the chair again, and this time, you certainly must feel something happening as you sit in the chair—a deepening of your relaxation and a very large energy within you and all around you. The reason you made the deal with the chair is simply because you made a deal with yourself—a deal to serve yourself in all ways imaginable, in all ways that you can. Because, let's face it, during your lifetime, and in every day of your life, you are in somewhat of a rat race. You lose sight of what you are really all about. By doing this and making this deal, you will be serving yourself, even though you are in this rat race society at this moment in time. You will always have the opportunity to sit in the chair when you want to, at any time you want to. Know this. This is a good thing if you would like it to be this way—a very good thing.

You Know Everything

Here is a twister for you. There is no real unknown, because you know everything. Many times people say the future is the unknown. It is really not the unknown. Your future isn't here yet, so you can't not know what it is all about until it gets here to you now. When it arrives in the now, you know it, so there is no unknown. Deeply within you and within your higher self you do know everything. If you think something is unknown, sit in the chair and ask your higher self to bring to you the aspect of you that deals with knowns and unknowns in life. Ask that aspect of you to change all the supposed unknowns into knowns for you so you can know everything, or at least have a good idea of what is to come, or what will take place, or what can take place for you, or what your future holds. You will have at least an idea, or you will absolutely know it, and don't forget to thank that aspect of you. To fear the unknown is to fear something that hasn't happened yet. Why put your energy into that?

If you think about your future and you have a bit of fear because it is unknown, sit in your chair and ask your higher self to bring to you the aspect of you that deals only with future events and future time. Ask it to explain to you the unknown of the future and how you can deal with it as being a known right here and right now, before it comes to you — before the future arrives as your "now moment." Set up the foundation and begin dealing in this "now moment" in time. Deal with your future in the "now moment." You will be creating your future, and then certainly nothing can be unknown.

You will have the assistance of that aspect of you to guide you through what you imagine to be unknown. If you can imagine it to be unknown, certainly you can imagine it to be a known to you, and something that is known to you is no longer an unknown. Get it?

Now, sitting in the chair, feeling more power, feeling larger energy, the news is, the chair is really your higher self. You have placed yourself within your higher self simply by sitting in the chair. Your higher self can be anything. It can appear in any way. You can have it be anything, any form, any shape you would like it to be. It can even be a duplicate of you that you can talk to face-to-face. Your higher self is simply more of what you are really all about. Every time you take your focus off, and away from, what you are every day, and you get more creative, and have more ideas, you are accessing your higher self. I think this bears repeating. *Every time you take your focus away from what you are every day, and get more creative, and have more ideas, you are accessing your higher self.*

How do you channel your higher self? When you have a new idea or an inspiration, get up and do something with it. This is how you channel your higher self. There is another way of channeling your higher self — having information coming to you that you don't recognize, or you are not familiar with. This could be for you, or it could be for someone else. Why? Because your higher self is also an energy point to the universe. Through it can flow all the information found in the universe, if you *let* it. You must let it, and you must *allow* it.

> **Every time you take your focus away from what you are every day, and you get more creative, and have more ideas, you are accessing your higher self.**

At times, you might be in the experience of all this information coming to you, and then all of a sudden, you will think, "Wow, maybe this is just my imagination." What is your imagination? It is what creates your reality. It is really your imagination that creates your entire lifetime. It is really, what creates your universe as well. Your higher self is also a part of your imagination and vice versa. All information comes from your imagination, from your higher self too, and through your higher self, plus your imagination. Everything works together all the time.

When you go to sleep at night, you can begin your sleep and dream time by sitting in your chair before you fall to sleep. Simply ask your higher self to bring to you the aspect of you that deals with sleep and dreams. Ask that aspect to please bring to you dreams of a creative nature that will help you throughout the rest of your lifetime so you can wake up and create your day. You can also go to sleep and create your sleep and dream time, which will also turn around and serve you by creating and recreating the rest of your life for you.

> **Ninety percent of what you have been taught, you will never use. It means nothing to you. You might as well throw it all away and simply begin brand new—if you want to.**

Many times, you will feel emotions that will be a bit foreign to you. Do not try to figure them out. Leave them alone. They know what they are doing. Let them be. They know how to express themselves, and it would be a good idea for you, if you would like to, to draw your emotions when you feel them. Draw them on paper. Often, you will confuse your emotions. You might feel fear when you are really feeling strength or secureness, and many times, you will feel doubt or sadness when you are really feeling happiness, or again, security, but you may doubt the happiness and security. This is because you have been taught many things throughout your lifetime and ninety percent of what you have been taught, you will never use. It means nothing to you. You might as well throw it all away and simply begin brand new. Throw it all away, if you want to. It means very little.

What you do use is what you are and how you are NOW. The emotions, the intelligence, the higher self, and all the aspects you are dealing with in the NOW are always in this "now time," even though they are in other dimensions.

Your higher self is more of what you are all about. It is always functioning in this "now moment," because this moment in time is really the only real experience you can ever have in your lifetime or in any lifetime. As long as this "now moment" is the only real experience you will have, why not really make the best of it? That means getting off the sofa, quit being lazy, and do something. Do something with your ideas, because they are all good ideas, no matter what they are, how small or how big. They are all good ideas. Do something with them. Have you ever had an idea, and then someone else comes up with the same idea down the road and makes a million dollars from it? That could have been you. You can have great ideas all day long, and what does that mean? Put your ideas into action. Do something with them.

Channeling your higher self means you are communicating with yourself on more levels of your awareness, and you are bringing forth and directing more of yourself. This is what channeling the higher self is all about—bringing forth and directing more of you. All those aspects of you are very real. They are very real. They are your personalities, your emotions. Some of them will be connected with a part of your actual past lives, some of them will be future lives, or connected with or attached to, your future lives.

The higher self is always to serve you. You are always to let the higher self serve you, if you want to. Everything is a choice. Letting your higher self serve you is also a choice—A GRAND CHOICE. If you make the choice to do so, you will be able to guide yourself through your life with more ease. Your life can be simpler and less complicated when you let it be that way. You are your higher self. Your higher self is you. All aspects are aspects of you, what you are now, what you have been, what you will be. You are always functioning as a complete unit. You are always functioning as a complete unit, no matter how things seems to be, no matter how your life might appear to be scattered here and there, to and fro—you are always functioning as a complete unit.

All you have to do to find your other aspects of your completeness is to use your chair. Ask your higher self to bring to you the aspects of you that deal with this, that, these, them, and those—you know what I mean—and they will come to you. They will appear to you. They will come to you and they will appear to you. They can only help you. They can never refuse you, because you can never refuse yourself. You can argue with yourself. You can fight yourself, but you can never refuse yourself, because you are always serving yourself in all ways imaginable. This is how it is. This is how you are. So, enjoy it. Talk with your higher self. Sit in the chair as often as you want to and enjoy yourself.

Chapter 6

CREATIVE VISUALIZATION

Now, we will discuss creative visualization and how you visualize. This is something you do all day long. Every time you talk, you are visualizing. When you say something, not only do you use words, but you are also using images in your mind and in your imagination. Your words blend with the images that you are seeing in your mind or in your imagination. Every time you discuss something, you visualize what you are discussing. There is really very little separation between talking, discussion, and visualizing.

The best way to visualize is by actually doing, participating in, and actualizing what you are visualizing.

There are a few different ways to visualize. Usually, when you take time to just visualize and not to talk, you see images in your mind just as you do when you are talking. At times, you might hold that image in your mind and focus on it, or concentrate on it, and, at times, you might see the image quickly. If you do, acknowledge it, and then let it go.

There is one more way to visualize. The best way to visualize is by actually doing, participating in, and actualizing what you are visualizing. Let us use an example. Maybe you have ill health—something isn't right with your body. You think, "All right, I'll use visualization to heal myself." So you sit and you close your eyes, and you take a couple of deep breaths, relax yourself, and you begin to form an image of yourself in your mind—an image that is all about health, perfect health, with no discomfort in your body at all. You can create many different scenarios with, and within, that image to cause healing in your body.

A Self-Healing Visualization

So, you begin to focus maybe on a cloud of energy surrounding your body and letting it settle into your body, and having the energy going to the area of ill health. One thing you can do if you are using this method is to see the area of ill health as being a blackened energy. Allow the cloud of energy, a pure white healing energy, to go to that area and see the color change from black to white. This is one good way to heal your body. If your mind chooses another color or shape for the healing energy, go with what your mind is showing you. Don't force anything.

The other way to visualize, rather than to focus and concentrate, is to *become* the process and participate in your visualization. If you are having ill health, as an example only, sit or stand and take a deep breath or two, and relax your body. See in your mind, and feel at the same time, a cloud of energy surrounding your body—a white, glistening, pulsating, healing energy. Feel it, and take your hands and move your hands around your body and feel the energy with your hands. As you are doing that, take your hands and direct the energy with your hands to the area of your body that needs the healing. You will be channeling the energy, the healing energy, through your hands to the afflicted areas of, or in, your body. As you are doing that, also see the blackened ill energy, the energy that is out of balance, and see it turning to pure white, glistening, pulsating energy, and become the healing.

When I say, "Become the healing," I am not only saying feel the healing taking place, but *become a new body*. Become a total new body. You know how you feel. You know how your body feels all the time. You know your body and have become used to the feeling of your body. This time you will become a brand new body, a brand new healed body. That means, with your consciousness, you will immediately change the structure of your body. Can you do this? Yes, you can do it very easily and quickly by imagining that you are wearing a brand new body. Your body has changed. It has become brand new.

You will feel this change taking place as you are directing the energy and having it change from black to white. See the healing energy as a white, glistening, and pulsating energy. You will feel your body changing. You will accept this new body as being your new healed body. This is how you *become* the healing. This is how you become the new body, the healed body.

After a few moments time of directing the energy, pull your hands apart. Feel the outer edges of your body, a couple of inches out from your body, and feel the energy still there. Feel the white healing energy still there. Acknowledge the energy, acknowledge the healing, give yourself permission to be healed, accept the healing, and leave the cloud of energy where it is. Relax your arms, relax your hands, and take one deep breath. Open your eyes and go about your day.

Depending upon what is ill with your body, and this is an example that you will have to repeat several times, because it will take the conscious mind a bit of repetition to acknowledge a change taking place, or to acknowledge that a change has taken place. Unconsciously and subconsciously, you are already healed, but consciously it will take a bit of time for the idea to settle into becoming a reality. Your conscious mind will want to revert to its old pattern.

When you have an illness, it has taken a long time for the illness to cause itself and become what you call a problem in your body. An illness will manifest when a problem has not been faced or resolved, and it will then become part of the identity. Most of the time, a person will focus upon the illness instead of focusing on the solution. Visualization is an excellent way to discover a problem and change the focus from the illness. It will not take a long time to heal it using this technique, but it may take repeated times of using it, and then you will be on the road to healing yourself. Realistically, you heal yourself every day with the words you use, the actions you take, the images you create and see. You are always healing yourself.

Remember, if your illness lingers, lasts a long time, or you have been told it is incurable, and you believe that, your illness is still serving you. The body can heal itself in a blink of an eye. Some call this spontaneous healing. Similarly, you are always causing yourself ill health, all day long, by the words you use, the reactions that you have, and the images you see and create. You may want to pay attention to how you talk, how you think, what you create in your imagination, and how you see it. Be aware whether you are taking action or having a reaction to something.

Now, back to the ill health. What your first impulse will be is to react in a harsh way. You will try to fight the ill health. Fighting ill health or a disease will only make it worse. Using the visual technique above, and being just all right with your ill health, will tremendously help the healing. What I mean is, you do not have to love your ill health, but if you can just be all right with it and not react to it or fight it, then you will be ahead. Fighting a disease only gives the disease energy — it gives it life and sustains it.

Other areas of your life, from time to time, will need healing also. Those areas usually will lie in your structure of emotions. Many times, you will go about your day with emotions functioning within you that no longer serve you, or emotions you can let go of, but haven't. They harm you in many areas of your life—finances, health, and all the rest. What you can do is create one more visual technique, and be very creative with this one.

Let us assume you are holding on to, hanging on to, certain so-called negative emotions. Negative emotions that are not serving you, and they are causing you harm—let's say in the area of finances. Something inside of you is keeping you from having the financial wealth that you deserve and you are due to have in this lifetime. You are due to have everything you want to create in this lifetime. Everything is your right to create in this lifetime.

Maybe there are a few emotions that are functioning within you that are keeping you from creating financial wealth in this lifetime. Once you find those emotions, and you will find them once you begin looking for them, because they are functioning brilliantly and may even be an old belief on top of emotions—once you find them and recognize them, simply acknowledge them and do nothing else but acknowledge them. Know they are there. Know they are functioning and know they are functioning brilliantly, and do nothing else for the time being.

Sit. Close your eyes. Don't lie down. Sit. Have a straight spine. Close your eyes, take one or two deep breaths and relax yourself. Become comfortable. Begin, in your imagination, creating a screen upon which you will project the emotions that have been functioning in, I will say, a negative way, keeping you from having financial wealth in this lifetime. Even if there is a belief, you will be able to project the belief onto the screen so you can see it with your eyes closed. Give form, give shape, and give identity to the emotions or the belief—and that means seeing them in any way they want to represent themselves to you. You are giving them the opportunity to show themselves within form to you. Once you see them on the screen, simply acknowledge them. Acknowledge their existence. Do nothing else at this point but acknowledge their existence within you.

Also, in your imagination, create an individual. It might look like you or someone entirely different. Project this individual upon the screen. On the screen, you will have the emotions, and maybe even a belief or two, and this individual. Now, visualize the individual walking toward the belief or the emotions, or all of them, and the closer this individual gets to the belief or emotions, you will visualize that he or she is absorbing the belief, or beliefs, and/or the emotions like a sponge soaks up water. He or she will absorb the emotions and the belief, and once that is complete, then allow the individual on the screen to simply fade from your sight and see a blank screen. Do nothing else for the time being. Just see the blank screen.

Begin to visualize the idea of money. You can have it appear as anything you want. Project that visual image on the screen so you can see it. Again, have it appear as anything you want. If this is hard for you, then just focus on letting it create itself with its own form. The idea of money will create itself with its own form and show itself to you on the screen. Once you can see it, then I would like you to feel its identity. Everything has an identity—

everything. Everything has, and is, consciousness. Feel the identity, feel the consciousness, and feel the energy of the idea, the idea of money. Look at the idea of money on the screen. Look at the form it is showing to you.

Begin to visualize yourself as you are, as you look right here, right now, and project that image onto the screen, right in the middle of the idea of money. Have the image be of YOU. See yourself as you are on the screen, in the middle of the idea of money. Then visualize the idea of money going into you, so you will become the sponge and you will soak up and absorb the idea of money within your being on the screen. Do nothing else, have no reaction, take no action, do not become excited or emotional. Simply do nothing. Simply see it taking place.

Then, what I would like you to do is visualize this image of you looking just the way you are now, walking off the screen, and have it walk right into you as you are now. I want you to feel the energy of that image of you with the idea of money in it. Feel the energy blending with your energy as you are right now. Once you feel it, let it complete itself. Take one deep breath, refresh yourself, open your eyes, let it all go, and go about your day.

This visual technique can be used one or two times a day, every day, for as long as you would like. Know that every time you use any visual technique, it will take practice and a few days for your conscious mind to accept it as a possible or probable reality. Possibilities, probabilities, lie within visualization. You visualize possibilities. You visualize probabilities and when you accept them, and give yourself permission to have them, then you turn them into reality. They become reality for you, a part of your identity, and a part of your immediate reality and surroundings.

> **Visualization is a very powerful tool you can use to set anything or everything in a right way, or to put something back on track.**

There are times you will feel out of sorts with yourself. Throughout life, people are trying to understand themselves, trying to create, form, and to have a relationship with themselves they can acknowledge and be comfortable with, so they can enjoy their life. Too many times, people become confused because they let outer influences get to them, because of all the craziness that is taking place around them. Too many times, people let it get to them, which causes a duality or separation within the self. You will become separated from yourself, and you will feel out of sorts, almost as if you are not sure who you are, or what you are, or why you are. There is a visualization you can use for this also.

Take a deep breath and relax. With your eyes closed, imagine yourself in a wide, open field of beautiful green grass and flowers all around you. Nature is singing and coming alive all around you, and you feel the aliveness of nature all around you. Visualize yourself in that field. See yourself in that field, and notice nature coming alive all around you. Now, visualize yourself talking to nature. Nature is consciousness. It is always listening to you. It is always hearing you. Visualize yourself talking to nature, and tell nature what you need in your life so you can always know who you are, what you are, and why you are. Ask nature to please keep away from you all the influences that affect you in a negative way. Ask nature, in your own way, and see yourself doing this—to supply you with only, and always, all things that lift you up and support you emotionally, to allow you to know yourself as who you are, what you are, and why you are.

At this point, ask nature what it is specifically that you need to do to allow this to take place. Visualize yourself asking this of nature. See it in your visualization, and hear nature telling you what you need to do to allow all of this to take place for you in this lifetime so you can know who you are, what you are, and why you are.

Listen to what nature is telling you. Nature will always tell you what you need to hear. Listen to what nature is telling you. When you hear it, feel the energy of nature all around you as you are seeing yourself in that field. Visualize yourself closing your eyes as you are standing in the field and allowing all the energy of nature to melt into you, to merge with you, to come into your being. Feel the energy of nature within your being. Once you can feel it, simply say, "Thank you."

Take one deep breath. Refresh yourself. Open your eyes. Let it all go, and go about your day. As you are going about your day, remember what nature told you what you need to do to let all that take place for you and within you. Then begin taking action with your life, with your reality, and within your life and reality. Do what you need to do.

A Visualization for Balance

Too many times, people don't know themselves, and when you don't know yourself, dramatic things can take place. When there is a separation of the being, often, drastic ill health will take place. When there is a separation, you become out of balance. Balance and having balance within your being will always, always, keep you healthy, functional, creative, brilliant, magnificent, and all the rest. When you suspect you might be out of balance in any way, use one more visual technique, which I'll give to you right now.

Close your eyes. Take one deep breath. Relax your body, and in your mind see the screen, the blank white movie screen. Now, project onto the screen two bars standing upright, bars that can be of wood, metal, or anything you want. Two bars. One will be white. One will be black. They are separated from each other; one on either end of the screen. When you see that, begin visualizing them moving toward each other, slowly. Have them move slowly toward each other. As they do, you might notice something happening inside of you, a feeling of familiarity. A feeling of knowing yourself, maybe in a different way, or in a new way. Have no reaction. Take no action at this point, but focus on seeing those two bars coming closer and closer together, one white and one black. They are getting closer, and then suddenly, and gently, they merge with, and within, each other, becoming one bar. If the color changes, let it change to whatever it wants to change to. Do nothing. Once the bars merge and become one bar, you might feel the energy of the merging taking place inside of you. This is the balance that you are looking for. Take one deep breath. Refresh yourself. Open your eyes and go about your day.

If you are using that visualization and you don't like the idea of bars, project on the blank movie screen two images of yourself, exactly as you are right now. Do it right now. Close your eyes and take a nice deep breath to relax yourself. See the blank white movie screen. Project two images of yourself, exactly as you are right now; one on either side of the screen, and see them coming together slowly. Notice that one, maybe the one on the left side, as you are looking at the screen, has no expression at all. Maybe the one on the right side, as you are looking at the screen, is smiling. Have them get closer, and closer, and closer, and closer to each other, until they merge with, and within, each other. When this takes place, you will most definitely feel something taking place within you — a merging within you — a new energy; a vibrancy and aliveness taking place within you. When you see it, and when you feel it, then visualize this new image of you fading from the screen, and the screen will again become a blank white screen. Take one deep breath. Refresh yourself. Open your eyes. Let it all go. Go about your day.

Visualization is a very powerful tool you can use to set anything or everything in a right way, or to put something back on track. When things are out of sorts, don't react to them. Don't fight them. That will make things worse for you. If you want to, be very creative with your visualizations when you use them. Create your own visualization of something that is taking place in a not so right way in your life, or in your reality, or within your body. Use your imagination.

Imagine you are going throughout your day, things are all going your way and everything is going right, but suddenly something happens and things aren't right. It doesn't matter what it might be. All of a sudden, you just know something isn't right in your day, and you would like to fix it. Again, don't react to it. Don't fight it. It will get worse if you do. What you can do is use a visual technique. This technique can be done within a few moments time. You will do it very quickly, and the more you do it, the better and quicker you will get.

A Quick Visualization to Set Things Right

Close your eyes, take a deep breath, and relax yourself. In your mind, visualize what isn't going right within its own form. Let it show itself to you with, and within, its own form. It will show itself to you in any way it wants to. No matter what it appears to be, simply look at it. Have no reaction. Take no action. Do nothing at this point but see it.

Now, acknowledge it, acknowledge its existence, and ask it what its purpose is in being in your day at this exact moment in time. Then ask what isn't going quite right and what it needs you to do to have it change its structure of functionality so it can become another right, or another positive, in your day. Once you ask it, it will tell you. It can only tell you. It cannot, not tell you. Things do not work that way. It can only tell you.

Listen to what it is telling you. Acknowledge what it tells you. Do not react. Take no action. Do nothing. Simply acknowledge what it is telling you and say, "Thank you." Let it fade from your sight and from your imagination. Let that form fade. Take a deep breath. Refresh yourself. Open your eyes. Go about your day.

You will automatically begin to do what it needs you to do to allow it to become a right, or a positive, in your day. Once you ask for something, and once you are given what you ask for, you won't need to do much at all with it to have it function. Things in life take place immediately, instantly, automatically, and naturally. Really. *It is you that places blocks and limitations.* No matter what you are doing within you, within your being, you will be doing precisely, exactly, absolutely, what you need to do to let the situation change.

> **Stress doesn't allow the brain to fire properly. The electrical impulses are slowed down. They can't fire properly and they short themselves out.**

Check within yourself. Is everything in your life going right and serving you for your highest good? If the answer is yes, then good for you. Congratulations to you. If the answer is no, then close your eyes. Take a deep breath and relax yourself. Create the blank white movie screen, and allow everything in your life that is not serving you for your highest good to appear on the movie screen in its own form. You will begin to see forms on the screen. See them the way they want to show themselves to you. Do not react. Take no action. Do nothing at this point. See all the things that are not serving you for your highest good. They might be emotions. They might be beliefs. They might be other people. They might be situations taking place in your life right now. They might even be energies of, or from, past lives. See them all showing themselves to you on the movie screen. There may be only one, or there may be many. See all of them. Now visualize all of them on the movie screen changing in their own form, changing in their own structure of energy. The change can be any way you want it to be. Just see the change taking place and know the change is all about allowing all those things to serve you for your highest good and support you emotionally.

Everything has, and is, consciousness. When you visualize and see something changing, it will change. When you give it permission to change, it will change for you. When you give yourself permission to have the change take place within you, it *will* take place within you. You will have the change within you. As you are seeing all those things, people, or situations changing within their own form, within their own structure of energy, see them, one-by-one, fading away. As they change, let them fade away. Take no action. Have no reaction. Just see it taking place. Once they are all gone, take a deep breath. Refresh yourself. Open your eyes. Go about your day and let it all go.

When you want to change something, add something to your life, or get rid of something from your life, use creative visualization, and as you are doing it, make it up as you go along. Be creative. Invent and create it as you go along.

Everything comes from your imagination. You do. Your reality does. The universe does. The fabric of the universe is made of imagination. Everything comes from your imagination. Allow your imagination to create your visualization techniques as you go along.

Visualization is a tool you can use to simply make your life much better. Use it and see your life change dramatically. Life is really very simple.

Chapter 7

THE POWER OF THOUGHT

How are you thinking? Let us look at that question. How are you thinking? When someone asks you, "How are you feeling?" you know exactly how to respond, because you know how you are feeling. Most of the time you do. Sometimes you don't.

When someone asks you, "So, hello. How are you thinking?" You may immediately wonder what they mean and begin trying to figure out how you are thinking. "What do they mean, how am I thinking? What am I supposed to say? How do I respond? What am I thinking about? I think all the time, but what do I think about? I think about many things, but right now, the question is *how* am I thinking? I have no idea how I am thinking." So, how are you thinking? You say it first. This goes on within the analytical mind. You don't immediately know how you are thinking.

This is a very simple question, and there is a very simple answer. How are you thinking? This statement, or question, may baffle you, because you are not ready for it. You expect to hear, "How are you feeling?" You know how to respond to that question by now. How many times during the day do you run into someone who'll ask you, "How are you? How are you feeling?" Many times. How many times do you run into someone who asks you, "How are you thinking?" Rarely. It stands to reason you don't know how to respond to such a question.

The question is simple. How are you thinking? *How* are you thinking? Your answer should be, completely. What do I mean by completely? How can one think completely? You may think you think in fragments or bits and pieces, or in scenes, or in scenery, or in discussion within your own mind, but where is your mind? What is the mind? Is it in your head? Is it throughout your body? Is it around you, or is it out in the universe where you only connect with it from time to time? You may think your mind is what you are completely.

You may say to yourself, "I am my mind – my mind is me. I think completely, and I think with my mind. I think with me, which means I am my thought."

You Are Your Thought

If you are your thought, how do you think? Usually you will find yourself having a conversation with yourself internally. This is how people think. You talk to yourself within. This is a nice way to think, but it takes a lot of time, and to think your way out of a problem just might take more time than it should, or can, take you. Usually, I will advise you to take the word *should* out of your vocabulary, because it is a judgment. I will tell you that nothing *should be*, and everything *can be*. Let us say you caught yourself thinking of something and when you were thinking, you were having a conversation in your mind, within yourself, internally. This is a very slow way to think, a very slow process of thinking and a very slow way to arrive at the result—a very slow, slow, slow way to take yourself through an issue, a situation, or a problem. Over and over again, when you think and talk to yourself, you think it out with words within yourself internally. You internalize your thought in that way.

Thoughts are not only internal; they are also all around you. Thought is energy. You know this by now. Energy is all around you and within you. It is everywhere. So your thought, it is throughout the universe. It is in, within, inside of, and around all people—everyone upon the earth.

Think of this right now—when you think a thought, everyone on the planet has that thought around them and within them. Your thought could have been originated by, or from, someone on the other side of the earth. Is it really your thought, or is it their thought—his thought or her thought? Whose thought will it be? "Let me think about this for a time. So, I'll think about it and I'll talk to myself about it. I'll internalize a conversation about whose thought it is. Does it really matter?" No. Because all people, all across the planet, think the same all the time. You might think you think differently, and in some cases you do, but you are usually thinking the same thought all the time. You can think a thought. You can have a thought. A thought can come to you on a conscious level, or it can just come to you. You can think it, or you can create it, unconsciously.

When you create a thought, or when a thought comes to you consciously, this is when you talk to yourself. This is how you think. You talk to yourself internally, within yourself. You have that conversation about what you are thinking. When a thought comes to you, when a thought originates in your unconscious mind, there is no discussion, there is no talking, there is no talk, and there are no words at all. You might see scenes, and they will flash through your mind very, very, very quickly with no thought at all. This is a quicker, clearer, and better way to think. When you think unconsciously, when you think like this, in many ways, you are taking time and bending time within yourself to fit what you are thinking about, and to fit your daily routine.

If this sounds confusing, think of it this way—when you have a thought, rather than thinking in words, think that scenes are flashing through your mind. Within an instant, your thought is done. Consciously, when you are talking to yourself about your thought, your one thought may last for a few minutes time. *When you think unconsciously, you are taking time and shortening or bending time to fit your thought.* Doing this, you have more time left to have more thoughts unconsciously. Is it a hard thing to think unconsciously rather than consciously? No, not at all. Does it take practice? You bet it does. It takes a LOT of practice, because people have become used to talking to each other. Everyone uses words. How many times do you try to communicate with someone else using only scenes in your mind? Mostly never, because you believe you can't do it—but yes, you can.

> **If you were to think to an animal
> with scenes and with emotion,
> you would immediately be
> communicating with that animal.**

You Can Communicate with Your Pets

You can communicate this way with animals. This is the way you can communicate with animals, and this is the way they communicate back with you. This is also the way animals communicate with each other. They think with scenes combined with emotion—scenes with emotion. If you were to think to your pet, or to an animal, with scenes and with emotion, you would immediately be communicating with your pet or that animal. Animals think, feel, have memories, and live in the present moment, but they don't reason or rationalize like humans do. If people were to develop the skill of unconscious thinking by communicating with pictures and emotions, there would be better and clearer communication with animals.

Okay, back to the unconscious mind. By thinking unconsciously, you are saving time and giving yourself more time to have more thoughts unconsciously. It takes a lot of practice to do this, and I'll say it again; when you think, you think consciously, and you think with words and by having a conversation with yourself.

Right now, I would like to ask you, how are you thinking? How are you thinking, and don't say completely. How are you thinking? Think about that for a moment. Think about that consciously. Have a conversation within yourself. "Gee whiz, how am I thinking? How *am* I thinking?" Now, think unconsciously about it. Let the scenes go through your mind at lightening speed and they will show you how you are thinking. How are you thinking? One more thing I would like you to think about. What do you think about thought? Are you baffled? If you are not—good for you. If you are— here we go again with a very simple question. What do you think about thought? You know what a thought is. A thought is only energy.

Energy comes in many, many, many different forms. So, what *form* are you thinking in? What do I mean by form? Think about the word form. What does form mean to you? A very simple question, and it has to have a meaning—right? People think everything has to have a meaning. This is how people communicate. This is how people think. This is how people act, react, and live their lives. Everything has to have a meaning. You do nothing that doesn't have meaning. Sometimes you think you don't attach meaning, but usually when you do something, when you think, when you act, things have to have a meaning.

What does form mean to you? It has a meaning for you. When you figure it out, then ask yourself; "What do I think about thought? What do I think about the form of thought? How many forms can thought take?" A thought can have billions of forms, which means a thought can mean billions of things to you.

Because of one thought, you can, and will, have many reactions taking place at the same time within yourself. This all takes place unconsciously. Of course it does. If it took place consciously, and if you suddenly became aware of reacting in many, many, many ways at one time, what would you do? You would think you were going crazy. How can you be reacting to all those different ways at one time? How can you do it? Can you do it? Sure you can. You are multidimensional. You are not of only one dimension. You are multidimensional. Therefore, you are existing in many dimensions, and you think dimensionally. This is also how you think—dimensionally.

Now, being you are in this present reality, you are always connected to, and with, every dimension of your reality, in your reality, and about your reality. You are also always connected to all of your lifetimes, past, present, and future. When you think a thought, you are thinking consciously, unconsciously, and multidimensionally all at one time. Not only that, you are reacting in many ways to that one thought at the same time. As you are reacting, you are also consciously and unconsciously, usually unconsciously, figuring out ways to understand, accept, and allow your thought. Now that you have been given too much to think about, think about this. When you think a thought, do you think a thought or do you have a thought? Do you think a thought or do you have a thought? Both. You have it, you think it—you think it and you have it—both at the same time. You cannot separate the two.

Simply, when you think a thought, this is what happens. Your consciousness extends itself throughout, yes, the universe. Throughout the universe. When you think a thought that one thought is traveling throughout the universe. Since that thought is traveling throughout the universe, will it continue going forever, and ever, and ever, and ever? In a sense, yes, but it will always come back to you. *It will return to you.*

Is there an ending to the universe? Yes, and no. No, there is no ending, but there is a point at which your thought will begin to come back to you. How long do you think it will take? Will it take hundreds of thousands of years, hours, minutes, lifetimes, or will it take seconds? None of those answers are correct because when you think it, it has already come back to you. Now, having completed this circle, your thought having gone through the universe and come back to you, has completed itself. So, when you think, you think *completely.*

Here we go again. Thinking of form, and assuming you have figured out the meaning of form for you, what *form* do you think your thoughts in? What forms do your thoughts take within you? How many forms can there be? The answer is, as many as you can create within your imagination. You know this by now, because you have thoughts all the time. When you think a thought, it goes throughout the universe—it comes back to you before you know what hit you. So, you think completely. What form would you like to think in? What *form* would you like to think in? Create a form. Form can be anything you want it to be.

Would you like to think in a negative form? Would you like to think in a positive form? Would you like to think in a creative form? Would you like to think in a free *form*? I would rather think in a *free* form.

To think in a negative form is all right, but it slows you down. To think in a positive form is all right, but eventually it will slow you down also. To think in a *free form* will allow you to have thought in any form you want within your unconscious mind, so you don't have to think with words and what you are thinking about. I truly hope I am not confusing you. If I am, think about it for a time. If I am not confusing you, then stay with me.

Thinking in form — and form can be anything or any way you want it to be — always has identity. *Form always has a will to survive and lives on, moves on, and has movement within. Form always has emotions, or an emotional structure, built right within.* When you think a thought, you are taking action within yourself just by thinking. When you think of what you want to do, the moment you have thought it, you have accomplished it within you. You have only to act it out around you, and that is called reality — and your reality is a thought. It is nothing more than a thought. You think it, and it is for you. It is with you, around you, and within you. You think it, and you see it.

Assuming you have chosen what form you would like to think in, now ask yourself how you would like your thoughts to be in the form you have chosen to think in? Thoughts can be any way. I would suggest you have free form thoughts, free form thoughts. Thoughts that really have almost no meaning at all.

Why would you want to do that and why would I suggest that to you? Because when you do that, when you have free form thoughts with almost no meaning at all, you are giving to yourself the opportunity to have a thought that bears little value at the time — at the time. When it bears little value, at the time only, you can't react to it. You can, if you want to, take action with it. Let's assume you are having a thought. Think about anything. Think of it in a free form way. Let it come to you with almost no meaning at all. Do it right now. Time is up. You have done it. You had no time to react. You had no reaction. You cannot have a reaction. What you can have is a sense of action taking place within you.

When you think in a free form way, thinking free form thoughts in your form, you can then have more excitement about what you are thinking. So, you think of something. Your thought travels throughout the universe. It comes back to you. You are thinking in your own chosen form. You are thinking unconsciously. When you think this way, what are you feeling? I will tell you what you are feeling. You are feeling not only excitement, not only aliveness, but you are feeling a sense of achievement and accomplishment, all at one time. When you think of something, the exact instant you think of it, you have already created it within you. This is how you think. You think completely.

When you think of manifesting something, you think of what you want to manifest. The thought travels throughout the universe and it comes back to you in an instant of time. You then have created, directly created, what you are thinking of manifesting for yourself. It is within you. You internalize your manifestation. You can feel it within you. You can feel it, physically feel it, within you. You feel excitement, aliveness, vitality, and all the rest ... but now what?

Now comes the hard part. You have to begin acting as if you have it.

"Oh, that's not for me."

Why?

"I can't act."

Oh, yes you can. You act all the time throughout your day. You are only acting on the stage of life. What do you do? What do you do to take that internalization and begin expressing yourself in such a way that you have it now? What can you do? How do you do that?

Think of the feelings within you. You know you have aliveness, excitement, vitality, and all the rest, and you are just bursting to tell people about your thoughts and what you want to accomplish, or manifest, in your life. So, do it. This is how you begin acting as if you have it. You tell people what you want to manifest in your life. Tell them. If they want to hear it, tell them two times. If they don't want to hear it, tell them seven times. Just express it to people. If there is no one around, no one to call on the phone, then look in a mirror and express it to yourself. Talk to yourself about it. This is how you start expressing in physical terms what you want to manifest for yourself, or your life, or your reality.

Once you verbalize what you want, you then set into motion the energies that know what to do to create themselves as being what you are trying to manifest in, of, for your life or reality. While you are talking to someone about what you want to manifest, what will you be thinking about? Will you be thinking about how brilliantly you are talking? How you are conversing? Will you be thinking, "Gee, do I sound silly? Am I boring this guy, this girl? Do I really know what I'm talking about?"

You will have many thoughts racing through your mind at one time, and when you begin paying attention to them you will wind up in one state — the state of confusion. This is where practice comes into play.

Before you begin talking to a friend or someone, maybe you would like to begin talking to yourself in a mirror when you are all alone. Talk to yourself about what you are going to manifest. Tell yourself what you want to manifest, and talk to yourself as if you have already manifested it in your life.

"Hello, vision of me in the mirror. I would like to manifest, oh, a brand new automobile. Yes, I would like to manifest a brand new automobile. Hello vision of me in the mirror, I am manifesting a brand new automobile. I am in the act of manifesting a brand new automobile. I am in the act of manifesting a brand new automobile. I have manifested a brand new automobile. It's inside of me and I'm telling you about it. I'm giving it the opportunity to create itself in physical terms in my reality."

This is what happens to the energy when you think and when you think about what you want to manifest, and when you talk to yourself and express yourself. The energies that you put forth, that you set into motion, will take on a will to live — a will to have movement, a will to move on, and a will to survive. They have identity and they take on their own emotionality.

There are many ways to think. I have a question for you. How do you think about thought? Here we go again. It is a simple question. What do you think about thought — how do you think about thought? Do you think about thought? How? In a conscious way, unconscious way, subconscious way, hyperconscious way, superconscious way, god-like way? How do you think about thought?

How do you think? The answer is that you think within yourself. You think outside of yourself. You think throughout the universe. This is how you think. How do you think about thought? What is thought?

"It is energy."

How do you think about energy?

"Ever expanding."

What else?

127

"Always in motion."

What else?

"Something I create to serve me."

This is how you may think about thought.

Today, you have had many thousands of thoughts running through your mind and your being. There were a certain few that really excited you. All the rest, you can live without. They mean nothing. Take those thoughts that really excited you. Think of them right now, if you can remember them. Think of them right now. If you can't remember, then think of something right now that really excites you. It can be something you want. It can be something you don't want. It can be anything. Just think of something that really, really excites you. Now, take that thought and imagine you are, in physical terms, projecting it throughout the universe to the end of time. Do it right now. It is already at the end of time.

Where and when is the end of time? Is there an end of time? There is and there is not. There is, because time, for you, will end many times, many times, and many times over. There is not an ending to time, because time becomes space, space becomes emptiness, and emptiness is always there. You can't get rid of emptiness. It is always present. ALWAYS. Emptiness is really the place inside of you in which your thoughts originate. The emptiness is found in between what you consider to be your thoughts.

If this is confusing you, think of yourself sitting very quietly, closing your eyes, taking a deep breath, relaxing yourself, and beginning a time of meditation. Suddenly, you find yourself not thinking, and you surprise yourself that you weren't thinking. It is when you are *not* thinking that your thoughts and creations come alive. When you are not thinking is when your thoughts and *creation itself* will come alive. How can it be? If you are not thinking, how can you have a thought? Very simple; when you are not thinking, you become the emptiness that is the real All That Is, which contains all thought, because emptiness contains everything, just as if you were to throw away everything you have learned to this point in your life, you will have nothing, which is everything.

**When you have nothing, you have
every opportunity to create anything
or everything in any way you want.**

When you have nothing, you have every opportunity to create anything or everything in any way you want. This is everything. So, in nothingness, you find everything.

In emptiness, you find all thought. Emptiness is not really a void. A void is something without, but a void still has energy and life. There is energy to a void. It takes energy to create and make a void. In many ways, human beings are a void. This isn't being said in a negative way. In many ways, you are a void. Your energy becomes a void throughout your day.

From time-to-time throughout your day, you become a void. You need to become a void to refresh your being, to gather information, to have more thoughts come to you. To function unconsciously, you become a void, which is a good thing. This *is* a good thing. You do it many times throughout your day, and you don't even have awareness of doing it.

If you were aware of becoming a void, you may think, "Oh my God, I just died!" This is what you might think. Then you would startle yourself out of having the opportunity of being a void for a short time. You would end that experience, and you would snap yourself back to physical reality. Then you would be spending too much time in physical reality and not enough time in a nonphysical state of being, or as, or in, a void. This is balance. You need time in physical form. You also need to spend time in nonphysical form, or as a void.

> **When you are not thinking, you become the emptiness that is the real All That Is, which contains all thought, because emptiness contains everything.**

This is one more reason why you create the dream state — to create a void of yourself within yourself in which you can design your reality, figure it out, and begin to actualize it, so when you awaken, you will begin having new ideas and new thoughts about your reality. "Hey, I just had a new thought. It came to me out of nowhere. Son-of-a-gun, I wish that would happen more. I like it. I felt energized and good about myself."

It happens all the time. Just begin paying attention to yourself a bit more. That is all. Just set aside everything that is not serving you and pay more attention to yourself. This is all you have to do.

At this point, ask yourself, "How am I feeling?" You might think, "Well, I'm feeling pretty darn good right now." If you are, good for you. You might also be thinking, "Well, I'm feeling a bit confused or uncertain right now." If you are thinking that way, good for you. That will spark you into figuring out what I have been talking about all this time. Think about what I have talked about. Think *about* thought. *How* do you think about thought? Think about that also. *What* do you think about thought? Think about that.

What form would you like to think in? Think about that. It can be negative, positive, or free. Free form. Also, think about the next time you are having a thought. Would you like to internalize it as another conversation and take up more time and energy, or would you rather have it be in your unconscious and present itself to you as a very rapid series of scenes flying through you?

When you do that, in that way, you are having more of an understanding of your thought than when you think about it, because when you think about it and have that conversation within yourself, the internal conversation, you begin to analyze what you are thinking about. Then you will lose sight of its pure, true, creative force and energy. Allowing it to fly through you, through your being, through your mind, as a rapid series of scenes, or even only one scene, you will have more of an understanding of your thought. You will grasp your thought more quickly. It will mean more to you. It *will* have more meaning to you.

Now, I suggested to you to have thoughts that have almost no meaning at all. This is when you will find the meaning in your thoughts—when you have them represent themselves, show themselves, as scenes flying rapidly through you. This will mean more to you than thinking and talking to yourself about what you are thinking, and if you are thinking about something worth thinking about. Quite often, you think about things you really don't even need to be thinking about, or considering. You waste much of your time.

Quit thinking with your analytical mind and think with the unconscious mind. Let your conscious mind rest. It has enough of a job throughout your day just keeping up with you. Think more with, and in, and within, the unconscious mind. Let the scene, or scenes, fly through you. You will understand your thought in a much clearer, comprehensive way. It will have more meaning to you.

When you think, no matter what you are thinking about—and I will say it again—when you think, no matter what you are thinking about, and no matter how you are thinking, think in the grandest way you can. Especially when you think about yourself, your potential, and your abilities — think in the grandest way you can. When you think about your abilities, don't — and here we go again — don't talk to yourself within yourself about your ability. "Well, I have this ability. I know it's a good one. I'm thinking about it. I think I can do this. I think I can do that." Quit doing that. You do it repeatedly. You tire yourself out with the way you think. Stop thinking that way.

When you think about your abilities, feel; simply feel the energy within you. Feel the energy of your ability, or abilities, within you. When you do that, when you can feel the energy of your abilities, they will show themselves to you as those rapid scenes flying through your being. Then you will have more understanding of your ability, and you will understand yourself more and more.

Always remember; when you think, you think completely. You cannot think in any other way. It is impossible. Even though everything is possible, impossibility is also a possibility. When you are lying in bed ready to go to sleep, allow yourself to have one grand thought. Don't verbalize your thought within yourself. Don't have a conversation within yourself about your thought. Allow the thought to show itself to you as a scene or a series of rapid scenes flying through your imagination.

Let your thought be as grand as you can imagine it to be, and when you think of yourself, think of yourself in the grandest way you can imagine, because that is how you truly are.

That is the nature of your being—GRANDNESS!

Chapter 8

THE LAW OF ATTRACTION

The law of attraction states: *like attracts like.* If that is the case, then how could opposites attract? Opposites always attract each other into each other's reality for the sake of balance. The universe is and has a balance. Everything and everyone in the universe, and all universes as well, will have, and will be, balance. You will be a balance. You are a balance of positive and negative poles of energy. You are, as you are right now, made up of many imbalances and opposing forces within your own structure. Opposites attract to create a balance and to create a whole, a whole being, a total complete being — completeness.

Within you are opposing energy forces of positive and negative from and with which you will create your emotions. Your thoughts will then channel your emotional energy. When you have thoughts, you will have an emotional response to what you are thinking. When you allow the emotional energy its freedom, it will eventually create what is called reality.

You know by now that reality is, in a sense, the wrong term. To speak in terms of right and wrong for a moment, it is a wrong term because it is something that is not real. You know this by now. It is unreal. It is imagination. It is an illusion and an idea. When you think, you imagine. When you think and when you imagine, you have an emotional response that takes place within you, and many times you will think a positive thought, and your reaction emotionally will be a negative reaction. You do this many times throughout your day to create a balance within your being, to have balance within your being. Everything is balance.

The Law of Attraction is balance. Reality is balance, illusion is balance, and imagination is balance. Everything *is* balance. Everything *has* balance. Using your imagination, you can create any type, or any sense, of what you term reality that you would like to have for yourself. You can have anything you want. You *can* have anything you want.

Too many times you don't permit yourself to have what you want, so you don't have what you want, and you keep thinking that you want it. You would like to have it. You want it. You would really like to have it, but it never comes and you continue to want it. You want it. What you need to do is begin telling yourself you have it NOW, no matter what it is you want. When you think about it, or think of it, don't separate yourself from it. Bring it to yourself in the "NOW MOMENT." There is no time. There is only the illusion of time, because you separate yourself from that which you want and that which you want to do and will do. Since there is no real time, the only real time, really, is the "NOW MOMENT" in what you perceive as time.

Being that the "now moment" is the only real time, you can then have all the time you can imagine. You have *become* your thought pattern. You have created a certain way for yourself to think, and you think in that way over and over again, and you keep getting the same results over and over again. Maybe it would be a good thing to shift your thinking. If you slightly shift your thinking, just slightly, then everything will change. Everything *will* change, *everything* will change, every *thing* will change.

Don't think in terms of wanting. Rather, think in terms of having. It all begins within you and it all ends within you. Listen very closely, it ALL begins within you. It ALL begins within you. Maybe you think you know what that means, maybe you do and maybe you don't. If you did, if you really did, if you did know what that means, then you would have everything you have been wanting for, of, and in your life. Everything you have been wanting is inside of you.

I don't need to say this, but I will say it anyway. Everything is energy. Nothing is real. Everything is energy. Nothing is real. The energy is a part of your being. YOU are the energy. The energy is YOU. The energy is within you. Reality doesn't begin until you permit yourself to create from the energy.

> **Give yourself permission to have everything you want.**

At times, you might think that might be too much. Why should you ask for all those things? Why should you have all those things? Maybe you

137

are being selfish. Maybe it is not a good thing because maybe you are supposed to be spiritual, and being spiritual you really shouldn't have the material. They don't blend, they don't mix, and to that I say, it is your right to have what you want. *It is your right to have everything you want.* It is really all right to have what you want. It is okay to have what you want. It is all right.

If you are playing the game of not being deserving, not being worthy of—end that game. If you want to, quit playing that game and simply create a new game. How? By shifting, just slightly shifting, your thinking. Shift your thinking slightly to create and begin a new game. A game that states that yes indeed, you are worthy of everything, and you are, because everything is your creation. Everything is your creation. You create everything. You create the attraction to things, people, situations, and ideas that come to you. You create the attraction of opposites to you also. Like attracts like, and opposites attract also. There must be a balance within you. There must be. This is what life is all about—balance. This is what knowledge is all about—balance. This is what awareness is all about—balance. You are awareness, you are consciousness, you ARE balance.

Technique To Create Healing And Balance

How do you keep yourself balanced? By allowing yourself to do everything you want to do and to have everything you want to have. If you want to be spiritual, be spiritual. If you want to create material things, create them. It is all right to create them. If you are a spiritual being, good for you. Be that way, if you want to. If you have material things, good for you. Keep them and create more. It is all right. You will always create balance in one way or another within you, but there will be times when you are out of balance, and when you are out of balance your energies do not function properly. They might slow down, and the more they slow down the greater chance you will attract illness to you. You attract it. You create it.

If you wish to have a healthy balance within you, then close your eyes, take a deep breath, and in your imagination—because it is all imagination—in your imagination, create an image of yourself just as you are right here and right now, but with a slight variation to it. The image of you will be standing firmly, very straight, very tall, and the image of you will have an aura around it, and in the aura you will find all colors at one time—all colors at one time—not white, but all colors at one time. You can see them. You can feel them. You can hear them, and this image of you is radiating an energy that will go throughout the universe, affecting everything and everyone in the universe, and that energy will come back to the image of you that you are creating right now in your imagination. Everything is imagination. Take a deep breath, open your eyes.

What you have just done, is healed your body. You have just healed your awareness, your consciousness, and your emotional state of being. It doesn't take much at all to create balance or healing. What you have just done with that short, sweet, and effective exercise, is you have completely changed the structure of your being-ness right here and right now. Maybe you can feel the change within you. Maybe it is hard for you to feel it. Either way, simply know you have just changed yourself completely. *What you will do with that change is up to you.* You can either allow it to continue to take place repeatedly within your being-ness, or you can let go of it and go back to the same old and usual you. Either way will be fine. It will be up to you.

When you imagine yourself that way, you completely change the structure of all of your emotions. You change the structure of your conscious awareness, and you begin thinking about yourself in a different way, a more positive, creative, constructive way. When you do that, everything else will change. Once you allow one thing to change, everything else will follow along and change as well.

Your thoughts, emotions, and imagination work together to form your reality.

Everything begins within you. Everything is inside of you. The energy of everything is within you, because you are the energy of everything. You think of everything for yourself, for your life. Everything exists in your thoughts, in your emotions, and in your imagination. Thoughts, emotions, and imagination work together to form reality. Again, you can have anything you want.

You can have everything you want, if you want to. So, think of one thing that you would really like to have in your life right now. Think of it and close your eyes — no, leave them open, wide open, and imagine, with your eyes open wide that you have that one thing in your life right now. Imagine it, and as you imagine it, I want you to get to know it. Feel it. Touch it. Hear it. Smell it. Let it be as alive as you can let it be.

Feel the energy of it within your body. Feel the energy within you. Let the energy be inside of you and feel it. Don't channel the energy. Don't manipulate the energy. Let it do what it wants to do within you now. Let it do what it wants to do, because it will anyway. If you can feel the energy, you are doing a good job. You are on the right track to having everything you want.

If it is hard to feel the energy — since everything is imagination — imagine you can feel the energy. Pretend. Pretend it. Everything is a game. You pretend your game. Begin pretending your reality. Pretend your reality. Do you understand what that means? Pretend your reality. Pretend you are breathing. Pretend you are alive. Pretend you have a physical shell — a body. Pretend you wear clothing. Pretend you eat. Pretend you sleep. Pretend you bathe. Pretend you drive. Pretend you walk. Pretend you have your job. Pretend everything. Begin to pretend everything.

How can you have a real solid life and pretend it at the same time? This is a problem that people have created for themselves constantly. You can't see the real you or the real reality, because you have created a false you and a false reality. You continue to function in what appears to be real—what you think is real. If you think it is real, then maybe you are already pretending it is real. If you would like to, begin pretending everything. Pretend everything you do. Pretend you are doing it. If that is hard for you to understand, then break your thought processes down to their most simple form. Think in the simplest way you can. Quit playing the game of complication and play the game of simplicity. Let everything be simple, because everything *is* simple. So, let it be that way. People have the knack of pushing away from them that which they want for, and in, their life. It is all right; you can change it when and if you want to.

Technique for Creating What You Desire

Close your eyes, take a deep breath, and imagine you see two things you want floating around your body in a circle, around you. See two things that you want floating around slowly, floating around your body. Imagine now you are reaching out with your right arm. Your right hand is grabbing onto one of those things. Feel it in your hand. Bring it slowly and gently to your chest, and let it melt within you and become a part of you. Feel the energy of it. Reach out your hand. Hold on to the other thing. Feel it in your hand. Bring it slowly, gently to your chest, and let it melt within you and become a part of you. Feel the energy of it within you. You are now attracting it to you. In fact, you have brought it to you. It is within you and you have become the energy of it. It has become the energy of you. You have created a blending and merging of your energy and the energy of what you want. Once you can feel the energy of what you want within you, then use your imagination again, and begin pretending it is in your life and in your reality. Let it be there. Allow it, and let it be there.

You are the magic of life, and you create your reality, or the illusion of your reality, in many ways, not only in one way, but in many ways. You have many realities all around you. You only see one of them at a time, because that is how you have come to think and focus. Begin pretending, just simply pretend, you can see more than one reality at a time. Pretend it and the first time it happens, the first time you see more than one reality at one time, it may shock you. It may also startle you, and you might shut down the game and go back to seeing only one reality. What do you do then? You pretend again. Pretend you can see more than one reality. This is to get you to simply change your thinking. Simply change your thinking and change it in a simple way. Don't complicate how you change your thinking. Change it in a simple way.

Everything is nothing more than empty space. Everything. That empty space is also you. You think yourself to be solid and real, and so you are. You think your reality to be what you think you would like it to be, and so it will be. Your thoughts create everything. Slightly, just slightly, shift your thinking. Slightly think in a different way, just slightly, and everything will change. Everything will change for you when you let it. When you attract an opposing force to you, maybe a situation, maybe another individual, you think it might not be a good thing, but there is usually an excitement, a circumstance of excitability within that attraction. Something is going on. Something is taking place. You, within yourself, have been lacking what that situation, or individual, is bringing to you. You give that to yourself by creating the situation, or the individual, giving yourself the opposite or opposing force. It is a very easy thing to do to create and to attract to you something or someone that, or is, or who is, opposite from you. It is an easy thing to do. It is also an easy thing to attract to you what you want. Life is an easy thing. Everything is easy and everything is simple, because this is how it is designed — very easy and simple. The design is simple. People are the ones that make everything complicated and filled with drama.

Now, if you think in terms of God, then think God had designed everything to be easy and simple for you. If you think you are God, then think you create and design everything to be easy and simple for yourself. Not only do you design everything for yourself, you create and design things for other people and you attract them to you. You draw them to you, and in a sense, you use them for a time. When you get what you need or want from them, and when they get what they need or want from you, then you part ways and you create someone else, attract someone else, and they do the same thing. You are always attracting everything to you. Everyone serves everyone else.

"Then why am I not attracting enough money to myself and in my reality?"

Because one way or another, you keep pushing it away from you.

"Why would I do that?"

Maybe you have made money a bit too important, and maybe you have created a bit of anxiety about it within you. Why should you have all the money you want to have anyway? Who are you? What are you all about? You really do not deserve it. Many times, this is what you think with your internal chatter. Let me tell you that you DO deserve it. Precisely, absolutely, you deserve it. If you have created importance and anxiety concerning money, then think about money in a different way. It is only a game. It is only energy and only an idea. It is a part of your plan, your creation, and your design. Since it is only an idea and only energy, then begin letting it be what it can be for you. Embrace it. Embrace it as an idea. You CAN do this.

How To Create Money

Close your eyes, take a deep breath, and relax yourself. See money floating all around you. See it in your imagination. Reach out your right hand and begin grabbing onto all the money. Bring it to your chest gently, and slowly let it melt within you to become a part of you. Feel the energy of the money. Become the money. Everything all around you is made of money. Imagine it. Pretend it. Imagine when you talk, when you open your mouth, money flows out of your mouth. Imagine it. It is a game. Play the game. You will be drawing the energy of money to you. Doing that, you will feel less and less importance placed on money, and less and less anxiety about money. It will become a game. When things become a game, they become fun. When things are fun, they create themselves effortlessly. Play it all as a game, because it is all a game.

You have good health right now. You have all the money you want right now. You have everything you want right now. It is all within you. Your life is your design. When you begin acting as if you have everything you want, you will create it to be that way.

There really is no magic in life at all. Certainly, there are no secrets in, or to, life. Everything *is* known to you, and everything *has* been known to you. Everything I have said, you already know. It has all been within you. From time to time, you simply lose sight of what you know. It is all right. Pretend you know everything and you *will* know everything.

Let me tell you something. I tell you to pretend and it will be, because everything is just that simple. Can you sit and pretend you have a pyramid in the middle of your room? Yes, you can.

"Will it be there in physical form, immediately?"

No, it won't.

"Why? I thought you said everything is simple?"

It is simple. If you were listening, I also told you if you let things be, they *will be* for you.

"How do I let things be?"

You know what you want to do with your life. You know what you want to have for your life, in your life, and for yourself. You know it. Bring the energy to you in the "present moment in time," not tomorrow, not in three weeks, or two months, or ten years from now, but *now*. Bring the energy to you now. Feel it now. Act as if you have it now, and you will create it. You will also create things that might not be that good for you, and if you do, and when you do, then ask yourself how it is serving you, because everything serves you in one way or another. *Everything will serve you.*

"If I want something, do I really have to do something to have it?"

Absolutely you do. You know what you want. When you imagine you have it, when you act as if you have it, you will be taking the steps to create it. You really cannot sit and create everything in front of you immediately. You cannot do it, because you do not believe you can do it—not yet anyway—but you will.

As you attract the energy to you, as you begin acting as if you have it now, you will be taking the steps you need to take to create it. Wouldn't it be nice to simply laze away the day and create everything all around you, not having to move a muscle? Simply have a thought and POW! It will be there in physical form. Wouldn't that be nice? Not really. What would you do with everything you would be able to create in that way? What would you do with it? You wouldn't appreciate it. Once you really get to know what you are all about, you will begin to enjoy the opportunity to be what you are all about, and that is creating and recreating, over and over again. When you close your eyes and see something you want, it sure does appear to be real, but no, it is only your imagination. That is right. It is your imagination, because everything is imagination. Everything begins in your imagination. So, imagine it.

The Law of Attraction also states that you can have anything. You can have everything you want when you give yourself permission to have it. That can be a difficult thing to do. That can be a hard thing, because of the way you have been thinking about yourself for your entire life, to this point. Oh my, I do think we talked about shifting your thinking slightly about yourself. So tomorrow, not today — take today off from creating reality — and tomorrow, when you feel very ready and very creative, think one thing differently about yourself, just one thing. If you find it hard to think differently about yourself, then think about yourself in the old same, same old, old same, same old, usual way, but change it slightly.

Maybe you can think about yourself in the old, usual, familiar way, but with a bit more excitement. Think about yourself being dull and boring with excitement, or think about yourself being vibrant and exciting with more excitement. Just change one thought tomorrow, not today. Take the day off.

When you do change just one thought, I think you might want to do it again, but two thoughts in one day might be a bit too much. One thought a day — that is enough.

I am being serious with you. One thought a day is enough, and in a few days, it will become a habit, and every day you will have a new thought about yourself, and that is really all you need to do. All you need to have is one new thought a day about yourself, and if you have one new thought a day about yourself, watch out. You will unleash yourself and you will begin to realize what you really are — what power you really are. You may also stay the same. That will be up to you. Either way, enjoy yourself. Enjoy how you are. Enjoy what you are all about. Either way, enjoy everything, if you want to.

Life is a choice. Attracting things, people, and situations to you is a choice also. You can choose to do it or you can choose to not do it. That is your choice. Either way will be fine, but once you begin choosing to be something, to be some way different, you will want to do it again, because it will bring new emotional energy to you and you will want to do it again, and again, and again. Then you will be doing it all the time. Stop finding ways to push things away from you. That is an old game. It does not work anymore — not for you, not anymore. Stop playing that game, and begin allowing yourself to at least imagine you have what you want to have.

It all begins with your imagination anyway. If you can imagine all the ways to push things away from you, certainly you can then imagine ways to attract everything to you. Do you really deserve things? Yes, you do. Are you really worthy of having everything? Yes, you are.

Retrain yourself by imagining yourself being different. Look at all of your games and change the games that you want to change. It is just that simple. Can you do it? Of course you can do it. Are you allowed to do it? Yes, you are allowed to do it. Everything is right here and right now for you. I will say it again. *Everything is right here and right now for you.*

Do you like the idea of abundance? I know you do. Everyone would like to have abundance. That is why you do not have abundance, because you would *like to have* abundance. If you remind yourself that *you are abundance*, right here and right now, you will feel it, and it will create itself for you.

Quit looking at yourself as being stuck, because the more you look at yourself that way, the more you will be that way. Quit looking at yourself as not being able to move about freely within creation. The more you look at yourself that way, the more you will be that way. Begin looking at yourself as being a free creator, able to create anything. The more you look at yourself that way, the more you will be that way.

Begin thinking you have everything now, because you do. The more you look at yourself that way, the more you will be that way.

You really are not boring. You really are not dull. You really are exciting and you really are vibrant with life. You really are a powerhouse of energy. You really are. See yourself that way. The more you see yourself that way, the more you will be that way. *Be the magic of your own reality.* Yes, you can do it.

Never look at yourself as being less than. Always see yourself as being equal with, no matter what it might be.

Chapter 9

APPLYING THE LAW OF ATTRACTION

When you consider something, when you think of something, no matter what it might be, you have already begun its creation. It exists within you and the energy is within you. Then how you treat yourself, how you express yourself, will determine the degree of its manifestation in what you call your reality. If you can think that reality is an illusion, it can free you in many ways so you can become more creatively functional, and the more creative you can be, and the more you can do, the more time you will create for yourself. Really, you are never running out of time. If you think that way, change your thinking and begin thinking you have all the time you can imagine, because you imagine time. You imagine everything—everything is your imagination. EVERYTHING. It all begins within you and ends within you.

If everything is your imagination, and if everything is within you, what is the point of having a reality? Think about it. *Having a reality is having a situation and an opportunity in which, and with which, you can express yourself emotionally and creatively.* "But why?" I will tell you why. To re-realize yourself in a new way. You do this over and over, and, too many times, you are not aware of how you are realizing yourself. Too many times, you think you are just a physical human being going through the drudgery of life, many times having a good time, and many times having not such a good time.

Look at yourself. How many times have you had dreams in which there were other people? You could be doing things with them or you could be talking with them. Those people are you. They could be your past lives, but most of the time they are aspects of what you are all about now, and your dreams are your creations, and you use them as a proving ground for your reality. Déjà vu. "Hey, this is weird, I've done this before." Yes, you have done it before in your dreams. You have created it in your dreams and now you are acting it out in physical form—no magic—really nothing to it. It is just you re-acknowledging and re-experiencing yourself in another form. You do this over and over again. You do many things over and over again and you are not aware of it.

If you can, think of yourself in a slightly new way, a slightly different way as I have suggested. If you do, you will become more aware of what you think, what you believe, how you act, and how you function. Functionality is all about allowing yourself to be more creative. What do I mean by being creative? I mean *allowing* yourself to be what you are all about, and you know what you are all about to a degree. You have a lot to learn about yourself, and this is a good thing. You think you know everything. You do know everything, because it is all within you. It begins with you, it ends with you, and it will always stay within you, because you are everything. You create everything, therefore you experience everything within yourself and what is called reality, which is an illusion.

Let's think for a moment. *You are an illusion existing in an illusion.* What does that bring to you? Power. Being an illusion, you can be free of anything that will hold you down. Being an illusion can mean total and complete freedom to function creatively. Reality is an illusion. You are an illusion. It is all imagined, and it is all really a game. Can you think of your life as a game? Can you think of reality as a game? Can you think of yourself as a game?

> **You can change anything at any time.**

How are you playing your game? Are you winning your game or are you losing your game, or are you simply staying the same? Are you not winning, or losing, but just playing the middle of the road game? How would you like to change it? When would you like to change it? What is holding you back?

You may think that you don't know, but yes you do. Oh yes you do. You know everything, so quit playing that game. To change a game simply means writing new rules of the game and if the word rule seems harsh or confining, then you can rewrite the experience of your game.

"Yes, I like that word much better — experience."

Thank you. I thought you might. The word experience is more freeing, thank you very much again.

How do you see yourself from day-to-day? Begin noticing how you see yourself and how you think of yourself from day-to-day. What do you believe about yourself from day-to-day? It might be time to change how you see yourself, how you think of yourself, and what you believe about yourself. It might be time to change it. If you are perfect, with nothing to change, good for you. Rather than being perfect, I think it would be better to be perfection. Perfect means you cannot change because you are it, and perfection means you can have more added to it — it can grow, and grow, and grow. So, be perfection. You are perfection. Begin, if you want to, thinking of yourself as being perfection and begin seeing yourself that way.

Hey, I have an idea for you. Do you have a mirror in your home? Sure you do, but if you don't, buy one and put it somewhere in your home where you can go to it one time a day — no three times — no thirteen times a day. As you pass by it, smile to yourself and say, "You are perfection." Walk away, go about your business, and do that as many times a day as you would like, and do this every day, if you would like to.

Everything Is A Choice

Everything you see is a choice. Life is a choice, and you have chosen this lifetime in this time, your body, your identity, your parents, and all the rest.

You have chosen all of it, because you have created all of it. It is all your creation. When you are with people who rub you the wrong way, you created them. Why would you create them? *To show yourself what is taking place emotionally within you.* If someone is an aggravation to you, there is something taking place within your emotions that can use a change. Find it, change it, and you might be surprised. The attitude of that individual will change. Why? Because you have created that individual.

"Now wait a minute. Are you really telling me I create people?"

Precisely, so congratulate yourself.

"If I create people, do they create me?"

Now you are catching on, because now you are talking about co-creation. Are you thinking we are getting farther into the rabbit hole? Stay with me, I know you are following what I am saying.

You may have someone in your personal life, or work environment, that makes life miserable for everyone and rubs everyone the wrong way. This type of person may be very happy being miserable, and they enjoy spreading their misery to others. Let them have their misery—it is their choice. It is also your choice to react to it. Remember, it all begins within you. How many times have you heard you are the god of your life and your reality? A few times, and if you haven't, you just did. Think about that one, because you are the god of life—your life. You are the god of your reality; because you chose it and you create it. Since you chose it, and you create it, everything you think about will come to you. The law of attraction states simply that like attracts like. Really? What about opposites attracting? Everything is energy. Everything is identity. Everything you experience and create is *of*, and *from*, your identity, your awareness, and your consciousness. Opposites attract to fulfill each other, and to make each other whole and complete, and they become a part of each other to create balance. Like attracts like.

If you think of something, it will come to you in your reality. If you are in anger, you will draw angry people and situations to you. If you feel good, you will draw good things to you. If you *feel* money, you will draw money to you — not *think* of money, but *feel* money. You will draw it to you. To *feel* it is a bit more involved than thinking it. We will repeat the money visualization.

Give Yourself Permission To Have What You Want

Close your eyes, take a deep breath, and relax yourself. Begin to imagine a stack of money floating around your body in space, all around your body in a circle. Reaching out with your right arm, gently, and with love, take the stack with your hand, bring it to your chest, and feel the stack of money on your chest. Allow it to melt within you. Allow it to become energy and melt within you. The energy of the money is now becoming a part of your energy, and you are becoming part of the energy of money. Keeping your eyes closed, think of one more thing you really want. Imagine it floating around you, no matter what it might be. You may have to change the size of what you are thinking about. Imagine you are reaching out your right arm. Grab onto that which you want. Bring it gently to your chest and allow it to melt within you. Let it melt within you. The energy of what you want is becoming your energy. You are becoming the energy of what you want. You have given yourself permission, right now, to have what you want. Open your eyes and take a deep breath. If you like, you may do this exercise as many times a day as you would like.

To focus on something doesn't mean you have to sit and concentrate, and concentrate, and concentrate, and focus, and concentrate, and think about it, and concentrate, and will it, and will it, and will it, and focus, and concentrate. No. To focus on something simply means you think of that something, and the best way is with your eyes open. See it in your reality quickly, and allow it to be. Then let it go and go about your day and don't think about it. Do that as many times as you want to.

You *can* have everything. Change your way of thinking about yourself, and change how you think, if you want to. Think about how you are thinking and how it is keeping you from having what you want. Obviously, something is going on with you emotionally and in your thoughts, which is keeping from you what you really want. What could it be? Maybe you don't feel equal with what you want. Maybe you don't think you are worthy of what you want. Many people feel that way. Maybe you don't know what you want. That is very good. If you don't know what you want, begin creating in your imagination what would serve you in the best way.

All things serve you. All the good emotions serve you. All the not-so-good emotions also serve you. Everything serves you. Everyone serves you. Everything serves you. All situations serve you. Why? Because you create it all.

Do something for yourself. For one month, drop the importance of money, and do not worry about money. Do not think about money as being something you need. Start thinking of money as being something you can play with. If a month is too long, then do it for a week. If a week is too long, then you are just lazy and you need to rethink your vitality. One week or one month—just do it. When you do this, you will notice something changing. You will notice your belief about money will change, and more importantly, your belief about yourself will change, and you just might notice money coming to you. It is your creation and money is only an idea. So, think big!

> **Once you quit thinking and begin knowing, then you have won the game.**

See what you want. Focus for a moment on what you want—not for a long time. Focus, preferably with your eyes open so you can see it in your reality. See it and let it go. If you concentrate on it you will change things, and when you concentrate, you are allowing your conscious mind to work, because in your conscious mind is the analysis. Do not analyze things. Just see them and go about your business and your day. If that is how you are, analyzing everything, then maybe it is time for a change. If you really enjoy being that way, then be that way. It is all right.

You can be any way you like to be. You *can* be any way you want to be. You can everything. Have to? Throw it away. Must? Throw it away. Supposed to? Throw it away. You should? Throw it away. You CAN anything and you CAN everything. When you think you can't do this, or you don't know how to do that—think again. You can do it, and yes, you do know how to do it. Let yourself know how to do it. If you have a burning question and you really need an answer to your question, whom can you turn to?

Try yourself. I told you and I will tell you again. Everything begins and ends with you and within you. You have it all within you right now, and all the answers you seek. *Everything is within you.* EVERYTHING IS WITHIN YOU. Do you hear me?

Why do you think people are so stubborn? If you create stubbornness within you, how does that serve you? What does it give you and bring to you? If you can't answer that, let me refresh your memory. I think I have said this at least a few times, that everything is *within you.* If everything is within you, then you also have the answer within you. Imagine what you would say if you asked yourself why you might be stubborn. Quickly, what would it be? Don't think about it. Maybe you are not being stubborn at all. Maybe you are just firm in what you believe in. That makes it all right. Right or wrong?

If being stubborn is really only you being firm in your belief, then you are really not being stubborn. Right or wrong? Don't think about it. How do you *feel* about being firm? Do you feel you are right? If you feel you are right, then you just know it. You don't have to think about it and analyze it. You just know it. Congratulations. Once you quit thinking and begin knowing, then you have won the game. This is a good thing.

Too many times, people *think*, but it would be better if everyone practiced *knowing*. To know will allow you to become functional and become creative, more and more.

"How am I supposed to know when I really don't know?"

Oh hogwash! Don't play that game. You know everything, and I am not flattering you. This is how things are. When you stop your laziness and begin to look within you, which may take three or four minutes of your day, you will find what you need and what you want. Try it.

Why do you feel the way you feel? Maybe because you choose to. You know if you choose to feel a certain way, you will feel that way. If you choose to feel a different way, you will feel that way. When you choose to change, your reality also changes. What will it take for you to see the change? *Acceptance and allowance of the change and the ability to change.*

All of this is nothing new, and since this is not new news, there are no secrets to life either. *This law of attraction is really no secret at all.* Everyone knows about it, everyone has always known about it, and the real issue is, what do you do with it? You know what the law of attraction states and what it is all about. So what do you do? You apply it.

How do you apply it? What do you need to do to apply it? You need to BECOME it. You need to see yourself as it. You are the law of attraction. Let me tell you something you may have forgotten. You are the entire universe. You are the center point of all creation. YOU. You are the entire universe and you are the center point of all creation. It all begins within you and it all ends within you. Being the law of attraction will change everything about you, about your identity, about the way you think, about the way you believe, your reality, and everyone in your reality. When you think of something, you will draw it to you.

Think of something right now and let it come to you in your thought. Feel the energy of that which you are thinking of right now. Feel the energy. If you are having a hard time feeling it, pretend you are feeling it. Remember, it is only a game. Play the game and pretend you can feel the energy. Once you can feel the energy, let it reside within you and become a part of you. Once you feel the energy, you should be able to feel your own level of energy on the rise within you. You know down deep within you that you *are* the grand creator. If you really do not know it, maybe you think it. If you haven't been thinking it, begin thinking it and begin knowing it, because that is the way it is. That is the way you are. That is what you are all about. Everything serves you. Everything *will* serve you.

Why don't you have all the things you want? Because you push them away from you. You continually want them. You don't recognize, or realize, they are already a part of you right now. They are inside of you, in your being, right now. If you are having a hard time understanding that, if you are having a hard time having what you want, if you are having a hard time creating things, begin all over again. Take everything you have learned to this point in time, and get rid of all of it. Throw it away and have nothing. When you have nothing, you have everything.

"How can that be?"

When you have nothing, you begin all over again with nothing. You have every opportunity to be the way you want to be, to be how and what you want to think, to believe what and how you want to believe, to act anyway you want to act. You will not have judgment. You will not have any emotional patterns, so you are free to be what you want, have what you want, and create what you want— immediately.

Life Is About Service

Life is all about service. It is all about service. Your life is to serve you. Is it good to serve other people? Yes, it is a good thing. Serve people, but also serve yourself and do not let go of yourself for everyone else. That is not a good thing. Create and have the balance within you, and serve people and serve yourself. You deserve it, and it is your right. This is your life, your reality, and your creation.

When you try to force things into place, they will fight you. When you try to control things, they will fight you and get out of control. Allow all things to be. Everything is and has consciousness. Everything knows what to do. Everything will work itself out if, and when, you let it. You need to let your reality serve you, or I should say, you *can* let your reality serve you. You can if you want to.

"How can I?"

Let your reality serve you and quit forcing and controlling it. Instead, command and direct it. You know what you want, so command and direct it to be in your reality. Do not control it, force it, or push it into place. When you leave things alone and you let things be, they will work themselves out so they can fulfill their purpose in being, which is to serve you for your highest good. *Everything is to serve you for your highest good.* Always remember that and let it be that way, if you want to.

> **Serve people, but also serve yourself. Do not let go of yourself for everyone else.**

You are going through your life having fun from time to time, and maybe not having so much fun from time to time, thinking about what you can do from time to time, thinking about what has happened in your life, which is most of the time, and you continue functioning that way bringing the past in every "now moment" in time. Let go of the past and let it exist in the past. Do not focus on your future because that is keeping what you want from you. Rather, focus in the "now moment" in time.

If you have a plan for your life, that is a good thing. Have your plan, and plan things out for your life, but bring the plan to the "now moment" in time. If you have a plan so you become something or some way, do not plan it for next month or next year. Have it be now. Act that way now. If you want to change something about you, act as if it has already changed. Act that way NOW. If you want to be rich with money, act as if you are that way now, and that doesn't mean maxing out your credit cards. It is a game, so play the game. If you want to be rich with friends, act that way now. Be that now.

Sometimes you may be in pain, either from emotions or physical pain, and it is hard to focus. If you have health issues, close your eyes and focus on your body. Remind your body you are in perfect health. See an image of your body surrounded by a cloud—a soft, fluffy whitish cloud, and the more you look at the cloud, the more you can see it pulsating, and it is exploding. It is a cloud of energy. See that cloud going into the image of your body and see the image of your body standing tall, straight, firm, and radiating with a golden glow—a glow of health. If there are specific issues, do not worry about it. The cloud of energy knows what to do. The energy of the cloud will go to the areas with the issues and it will know what to do to begin the healing.

> **Do not fear anything. When you fear it, you will create it more quickly.**

Do not fear your pain or your illness, because you only give it more power. Do not fear anything. When you fear it, you will create it more quickly. Think of health. You would like good health all the time. This is something you can have. You can have everything you want, and this includes health.

Think of your health. Feel your body coming alive, and feel it tingling within. If you cannot feel it, imagine it and pretend it. Play the game. Feel the tingling getting very warm within your body, and let that tingling grow and spread to the surface of your skin. The tingling will be warm, not you. You will be just fine. Open your eyes, take a deep breath, and go about your day.

You Can Heal Your Body

When you focus on changing your health, and when you see that image of you changing, you are changing the structure of you. Your entire structure will change. Your energy will change. The patterns of your energy will change. *There really is no good health or ill health at all. There is only the experience of what you are at any given moment in time.* Let me repeat this. There really is no good health or ill health at all. There is only the experience of what you are at any given moment in time. There is only the experience of what you are — the experience of what you are, and what you are all about, at any given moment in time — which means what?

Your body is energy, and if it seems as though there is illness, or that something has gone awry, or not right with your body health wise, remember that first of all, you are an illusion. The illness is also an illusion. You can change and create an illusion. Therefore, you can change and create health when you want to, simply by having it be a different way. You are energy. Always be aware of yourself as energy, because you can change the form and the structure of energy. You can change it. If it seems you have ill health, give up your belief in ill health and give up your belief in good health also. Have no belief at all in health, if you can do it, and if you can give up the belief, your body will be any way you think it to be. Your thoughts and your emotions make you what you are, what you will be, and what you have been.

Creation, recreation, and life are very simple processes. People make it far more difficult than need be. Changing your thoughts about yourself is a very simple process also. Medications do not fix you, they do not heal you, and they have no power at all. It is your belief that they will heal you that heals you. *Your belief heals you.* Look for, and find yourself, a very beautiful rock. A small rock, and give that rock your belief that it can heal you. It is the same as your medication. I realize it is a very hard thing to believe that you can heal yourself.

Take your medications and follow your doctor's orders until you get to the point at which, and in which, you can *believe* that you can heal yourself, and you believe the natural state of the body is health. Follow your doctor's orders and take your medications, but realize you can get to the point of believing that your body can heal itself. You give your belief to that medication so it can heal you. You can cause yourself ill health, you can create for yourself good health, and you can change either one, and you can change both if you like. It is all up to you.

If you have a really good day, congratulations. You have created it that way. When you make up your mind about something, that something will be that way. What does it take to make up your mind? It is simply a matter of making a choice. You can choose to remain as you are, and that will be all right. You can choose to be the way you used to be and keep repeating that over and over again, and that will be all right also, if that is what you want. You can choose to change and be a different way, or a grand way, a more creative way, a more powerful way, and that will be all right, if that is what you choose also. It is up to you. What you think about, you will draw to you. What you focus upon, you will create.

I'll let you in on the *real* secret—the law of attraction is really a bunch of hooey because everything is an illusion. *You attract what you want to attract to you.* If you allow it, it will come to you because everything serves you.

Check your emotion to see how it is serving you emotionally. If you attract something that you don't think you want, it is because you need to examine something within you that is causing the attraction. It is serving you, so figure out how it is serving you. Check your emotion to see how it is serving you emotionally. It might be as simple as telling you not to do that again, or it could be a deep emotional issue. How deep would you like to go? Remember— *keep everything simple.* Do not dive deeply into your emotions, because it just might create confusion. May I tell you what your emotions are?

"Sure, go ahead. Please tell me."

As you know your emotions to be—anger, love, joy, and all the rest, they are judgments you place on yourself, something, or someone else.

"If I were to be without judgment, will I have emotions?"

You will have the power of your emotions all at one time, and you would be a powerhouse. If you think you need emotions, have them. If they are creating negatives, enjoy them. When you enjoy a negative, you get rid of the negative energy, and neutralize the negative energy. If you enjoy something, it can't be a negative. You enjoy all the positives, so keep it that way. How would you like to feel? Every moment in time, you are changing, and that means with, and within, every moment you can be better, and better, and better, if you think that way. You really ought to see yourself as energy exploding with life; pulsating as a creative force just waiting to be tapped to it is fullest extent. *YOU are an idea, and an idea can become anything.*

Chapter 10

THE LAWS OF THE UNIVERSE

The universe is a constant. It is a continuum. It keeps on going. It keeps growing. It keeps expanding, contracting, getting larger, and getting smaller, all within a framework of its own. Since there really is no space, nothing can get larger or smaller, but when an idea such as your universe has its own framework, then yes, it can do anything. It can expand, get larger, contract, and get smaller. It does this constantly, because *it is its own awareness and consciousness.* It sees itself as a living thing with a most definite purpose and a most definite reason to be. Within itself, there are many variations of itself. You can almost say there are universes within your universe, and in this sense there are. What lies outside of your universe will be many other universes as well, all within their own framework, and yet separate from your own.

The Law of Creation

As human beings, as a society, there are rules, regulations, and laws. Looking at the workings of the universe, it appears the universe has laws also. These are not really laws, but I will call them laws so there is an understanding and a reference point. Above all else, the universe has the most, I will say, important law of all, and that is *The Law of Creation.*

Everything is creation. Everything is a creation of its own in the universe and within the universe as well. Creation is a constant. It is a continuum, just as your universe. Creation will re-form itself over and over again, and recreate itself over and over again within its own framework also. When you create something, what you create will be created within your own framework as well, as you are precisely your own universe also.

> **Every action you take will be felt throughout the universe. Every thought you have will be realized throughout the universe, because you are your universe.**

You exist within the outer universe, and being that you are a universe, you are a part, a very important part, of the outer universe. You are of, and from, The Law of Creation. You have created yourself within the framework of the universe, and what you create for yourself you will create within your own framework as well. You can change anything at any time. You can change everything at any time you would like, because the universe is always to serve you. It is *always* to serve you. *The universe is always to serve you.* You, in many ways, had created the universe, as it gave you the opportunity to create yourself within it. By recreating yourself, in all the ways you can imagine, over and over again, you are adding to, and recreating, the outer universe as well. Every action you take will be felt throughout the universe. Every thought you have will be realized throughout the universe, because you *are* your universe.

When you think of creation, usually you will think of something coming alive or being born. There are many aspects of yourself that you have created, that you are creating, that you will create, that you will never recognize, or you will never realize. They exist within you and at the same time within other dimensions of this, your present reality, but you and all of them, all of those aspects of you, all of you together, are in sync. You are always in harmony within your own framework, within your own reality, and within the outer universe as well. Everything works together for one purpose. Everyone works together for one purpose, and that purpose is perfection.

> **Since the outer universe is within you, every thought you have, every action you take, every reaction you have, will have an effect upon you.**

The universe is perfection within itself. You, being your own universe, are also perfection within yourself, within your framework, and within the framework of the outer universe. There will always be creation. Without creation, you have stagnation. When you stagnate, you know what happens to you. The universe is always creating and you are always creating, even when you think you are not. You are always creating with every thought you have, with every action you take, with every reaction you have also. You are always creating. The universe is always creating. Together, you and the universe are always in sync, in harmony, and creating. ALWAYS.

The Law of Acceptance

Within creation, you will find one more law — *The Law of Acceptance.* What can you accept about the universe? You can accept that it is there, but where is it? Is it around you, throughout you, within you, past you, behind you, on the side of you? The universe is all over and within you. The universe is everywhere within you. It is within you. Those words are very important to remember. The universe, your outer universe, is within you. Why are these words important to remember? These words will always remind you who is creating what, when, and how. *The universe is allowing you to accept yourself as the supreme creator.*

The Law of Allowance

You can say there is a *Law of Allowance* also, and the two go together — *allowance and acceptance.* Allow things to be. Accept them and you will grow within your own framework as your own universe. By accepting yourself, you can allow everything within your own framework of your own universe. Everything works together all the time. Everyone works together all the time. Everything is everyone, and everyone is everything, because ultimately all there is, is thought energy. From thought energy, you have the *Law of Creation, The Law of Allowance,*

The Law of Acceptance, and with your thought, you have created everything you understand. You have accepted everything, therefore you understand, and in many ways within your being-ness, you understand that you can only allow.

Accepting and allowing are very important ideas to adopt within your life, your lifetime, and lifestyle. Accepting and allowing will eliminate the fighting, the warring, as all things are within you. Fighting and warring are within you, a part of you. Your thought can change that. Your understanding of acceptance and allowance can eliminate fighting and warring.

The universe has a most definite intention. It has a most definite intention, and that is allowing you to create and fulfill your destiny for yourself. Destiny is of your own choosing. You have made choices, but those choices are not your destiny. Your destiny is what you do with all the choices you have made and will make. Your destiny is your design and you can change anything at any time. You can change everything at any time you want to when you accept it and allow it. When you fight it, when you are at war with it, nothing will change. Only you will lose the game, the game of consciousness, the game of awareness, which is what you really are.

> **Your destiny is what you do with all the choices you have made and will make. Your destiny is your design and you can change anything at any time.**

You are awareness within your own form. Being that you are awareness, you really do know everything. At times, yes, it does appear you don't know or understand something. It seems that way. It seems that way, and when things seem to be a certain way, maybe they are not really that way at all. When it seems as though you do not understand something, look within yourself and find it. It is there within you. Everything is within you. The entire outer universe is within you. As I said, it creates and recreates itself within its own framework, which is a part of you, within you. Everything works together—everything. Everyone works together also.

The Law of Love

When you are creating with acceptance and allowance, you are then in realization of one more law of the universe—*The Law of Love.*

Love brings an energy. It causes an energy that will assist you. It will help you to understand what you are all about, what everyone is all about, what everything is all about, what your personal universe is all about, what the outer grand universe is all about also. Love is not being starry-eyed, throwing roses and blowing kisses. No. It is simply being within your own understanding of what you are. That is what love is.

When you are in understanding of what you are, then you can begin to love someone else, because you will understand what they are. When you repeat that pattern over and over again, you will find that you love many, many people. If you could understand the things that go wrong and why they went wrong, you would be able to love them, and then you would realize they are a part of you and your design. You would know they are a part of you and part of your design. Yes, you did create them. Everything and everyone that is negative to you—if you could understand the *why* of the negative energy—then you would be able to love those things, those people. When you love something, you negate the negative energy. It dissolves. It goes away, it fades away. To love is to understand. To understand is to love.

> **To love is to understand.**
> **To understand is to love.**

You want to create, so you create something. You accept it. You allow it. It comes into being within your reality. You understand it therefore you love it. You have love for it. You give it your energy, because it is you. It is a part of you. It is your creation. It feeds off of your energy, and in return, it will give you energy back. There is an exchange. Everything and everyone work together all the time. Everything and everyone, all of you and all of it, make up the outer universe, which is within you. It is all within you. *Everything is within you.*

To love yourself does not mean you must really, really like yourself and everything about you. No. You can be a very pleasant individual or a very unpleasant individual and still love yourself, love why you are, what you are, and what you are all about. To do that, all you have to do is understand yourself. Understand why you are the way you are. Why? Because you created yourself to be that way, based upon what you think you know about yourself. If you really allowed yourself to be in the experience of what you are, if you really allowed yourself to experience yourself, you would have grand, grand love for yourself, within yourself, and about yourself. Slowly and steadily, people are getting there. People understand themselves more and more every day, and this is a good thing.

To understand yourself is to understand the universe. To understand the universe is to be in touch with the All That Is. To be in touch with the All That Is, is to be in touch with yourself. The universe, as you know it, spirals through, within, and throughout other universes. You are in this universe, your present universe. You are also in other universes as well. The universe spirals through another universe, and in this other universe, there is another *you* where you are doing things very similar to what you are doing here and now.

When, and as, the universe is spiraling through another universe, you will begin to meet certain people. It may be a couple or a few at the most, and you will simply just know them. You will know all about them, and you will be drawn to them. They will be drawn to you. You are meeting yourself, but not necessarily appearing as you appear now, but you will be meeting, you will be seeing, and you will be with yourself. You recognize that with your feeling and with your instinct. You know what *everything* is all about and you know what *everyone* is all about.

The Law of Attraction

As you attract each other, think of the *Law of Attraction*. You attract to you what you need and what you want. This is your universe. This is your reality. The universe is within you. It is offering to you everything you need, everything you want. When you focus your attention and your intention, you create what you want. What you think of, you will draw to you. What you focus upon, you will create. Like attracts like.

> **What you think of, you will draw to you. What you focus upon, you will create.**

Opposites also attract to create perfection, to create a whole, a complete. What you lack within you, you will draw to you. You will experience that. You will have an understanding of what you lack, and in many ways, you become what you lack. Therefore, you will become whole. You will become complete within your own framework, within the framework of the outer universe, but as it is within you.

Please pay close attention to this. What do you think happens when you think of something? You emit an energy. You send out an energy.

Imagine it as a thread leaving you, not your head, not your toe, but your complete being. That thread is the energy. It is the thought, the consciousness that you send out when you think of something. That thread will go throughout the universe. Eventually it will return to you, but as it is going throughout the universe, it will attract to it other energies that will allow you to understand more completely what you want and why you want it.

As that thread of energy returns to you, as it comes back to you, you will begin to accept and allow its creation in your reality, in your framework, within yourself. How many thoughts do you have in one day's time? Many, many, many. Imagine thousands of threads of energy extending from you, reaching throughout the universe. Every thought, every thread of energy, is one more possibility for you. You have thousands of possibilities every day. That can be a bit too many for you to handle at one time, so focus upon the one that brings you the most comfort.

The Law of Transformation

You focus upon the one thing you really want, the possibility you really want to entertain. When you do, up pops another law—*The Law of Transformation.*

When you understand the possibility, you transform it into a probability. What do you think is the difference? A *possibility* is something that might take place. A *probability* is something that probably will take place. Reality is all about possibilities and probabilities. The energy of probability has matured from being a possibility. The possibility is, in a sense, a child. The probability is, in a sense, the adult within you. All around you there are thousands of possibilities taking place for you every day. Think of that—thousands of possibilities for you every day. So really, there is no reason why you cannot have all that you want. No one is stopping you. In fact, the universe is giving it all to you. You have only to really understand that which you want, and then create it. Understanding what you really want is the hard part. Creating it is the easy part. When you understand what you want, you can love what you want, and when you love what you want, you can accept and allow what you want. Then it will create itself for you within the universe, which is within you and within your own framework. *Everything* works together all the time. *Everyone* works together all the time. Everything and everyone work together all the time.

Being that everything is an illusion, everything changes so quickly that you cannot see it create itself. So how can you see it? I will tell you. Take a bit of time, sit or lie quietly with your eyes open or closed—that will be up to you. Take some deep breaths. Relax yourself. Imagine what you want for all of your life. Imagine it. If you can, see it in your imagination. If you can, feel its energy. If you can, begin to understand what it is, and what it is all about. Why do you want it? It might simply be because you want it and nothing more, and that is fine. If you can understand it, understand what it is all about, then you can love it. Then you can accept and allow it. Then it will create itself.

The Law of Change

Things change so quickly. You change so quickly. This is the *Law of Change*. There is always change. There is always creation. There is always love. There is always attraction. There is always change. You change so quickly you cannot see it. You do not recognize the change that is taking place within you with every moment of time until you slow yourself down, focus within yourself, and then you can begin to see the change.

When you are out and about in your world, doing your daily routine, going to your job, pay attention to everything being an illusion. If you can think of everything as being an illusion, nothing will invade, as you say, your space—as I say, your reality. Paying attention to everything being an illusion will allow you to focus more upon and within yourself. Not allowing an outer influence to invade your space, you can then focus within yourself more, and to know what you are all about and create more quickly, more brilliantly. Not being in or under the pressure of society will also give you the opportunity to understand yourself. Then you can love yourself. Then you can accept and allow yourself. Then you can create and recreate yourself, and you can see the change. Many times, you can feel the change, but you cannot see it. It is all right. That is a good thing. You are halfway there. Feel it, take the feeling, and close your eyes. Quickly imagine the feeling. Imagine the feeling, and it will show itself to you as the change. Then you can see the change. This too will take some practice.

> **You have within you the power, and enough power, to create, recreate, or change anything at any time you want.**

You are living on the planet. You *are* the planet. Your planet is you. Maybe you are thinking, "Well, I know that by now, so move on to something more interesting." Think, and I mean really think, if you *are* the planet, what does that mean to you? If you want to take care of the planet, that is a good thing, because it wants to take care of you. If you want to love yourself, that is a good thing. If you want to love people, that is a good thing. If you want to help people create their reality more brilliantly, that is a good thing. If you want to end all the wars on the planet, that is a good thing. Can you do it? Yes, you can do it. Yes, you can.

Let me tell you something, and you don't have to believe this. You can believe it or not. This is up to you. You can listen to me or you can zone out and think of something else. That is up to you, but I will tell you something anyway. You have within you the power, and enough power, to create, recreate, or change anything at any time you want. You have the power to end wars, end all wars—all the fighting within you. I will tell you something else. As the universe is within you, the planet is within you. Everything taking place on the planet is taking place within you. Even all those things you don't yet know of or have not yet seen. They are taking place within you now, because you are your planet. Your planet is you, because everything is energy — only and always energy. It is only and always energy. You know that by now.

When you end all your bickering with, and within yourself, all the fighting, all the warring that you do all the time, you have only one thing left within you; only one thing. This one thing can bring you everything you want, because this one thing will bring to you creation, allowance, acceptance, love, attraction, and all the rest. This one thing is peace of mind. You can change if you want to, and when you have peace of mind you are completely focused within your reality, designing your reality, designing yourself and your universe to the best of your ability with brilliance and with magnificence. Look at yourself as being the universe, the complete total universe. This is what you are. Everything takes place within you, everything. *Everything* works together within you. *Everyone* works together within you.

Yes, you also create people. Yes, you do. Don't believe it, or believe it. You create people. People use each other for a time, and then move on to create someone else. You use each other for a time to help each other out. This is life. It is a good thing. You want to serve each other, so you allow each other, and you accept each other, and you create together and that is co-creation. Everyone could, if they really wanted to, co-create one more reality within this reality. Yes, you can. Yes, you most certainly can. It would be all about what you wanted it to be all about. If you were to create a reality within your reality, I might suggest a reality of laughter and comedy. Every time you would enter this reality, you would laugh. All you would do is laugh—nothing else. You wouldn't think of anything. You would not act or react. You would laugh, only laugh.

The Law of Healing

Laughing will bring one more law—*The Law of Healing.*

Everything heals all the time. What, you missed that one? I'll say it again. *Everything heals all the time.* Everyone heals all the time. What does laughter do? Oh, not much except that it stimulates your energy, allows you to become more creative, raises your level of energy, excites all the organs in your body, recreates all the cells in your body, kills cancer cells in your body, kills illness in your body in a very gentle, loving way. So, laughter really doesn't do much.

There may be many reasons why you would want to cry. Every reason is a very good reason. You cry with joy. You cry with sorrow. Crying is a release, an emotional release, and from time to time, you need to cleanse yourself emotionally. Release the emotions. Cry or laugh. Either one or both, or begin crying and end up laughing, or begin laughing and end up crying. Crying is a good thing. Laughing is a good thing. Loving is a good thing. Creating is a good thing. Enjoying is a good thing. Being frustrated is a good thing, because it makes you think of possibilities. Anger is a good thing, because it brings you strength, if you allow it to, not weakness, but strength. Fear is a good thing, because it quickly gets you to being very creative very quickly. Everything is a good thing.

Listen to me. Everything is a good thing. Look at it that way, if you want to, if you can. Everything is a good thing. *Everything is a good thing.* If you look at everything that way, you will understand it *as being* a good thing, because you will realize that everything serves you. Everything serves everything else and everyone else also. When you understand its purpose, then you can love it. Then you can accept it and allow it, and it will create and recreate itself over, and over, and over again in your reality, which is within you.

You have your own uniqueness. You are unique within your own understanding of what you are. Allow yourself a bit more. Let yourself a bit more. Every time you allow and let yourself a bit more, you will expand within the awareness of what you are. You will understand yourself a bit more. You will create a bit more, you will be a bit more, and so will your universe and the outer universe.

Every thought you have, every action you take, every reaction you have, is felt and realized throughout and within the outer universe. Everything you do will have an effect upon the universe. Every thought you have will have an effect upon the universe. Since the universe is within you, every thought you have, every action you take will have an effect upon you. I will say it again. *Since the outer universe is within you, every thought you have, every action you take, every reaction you have, will have an effect upon you. Think how you want to be and you will be that way. Think how you don't want to be and you will be that way.* It is up to you. How do you really want to be?

You really want to be as the universe is — creative, accepting, allowing, loving, attracting. That is how you really want to be, within you. It is how you are. You need to see yourself that way and become more like the outer universe.

Things are changing. Things are mounting up, and people need to calm things down now. End the fighting, the bickering, and the warring within. End it. Please end it. Please begin working together.

You need to do this. You need to do it now. Everything IS an illusion. Yes, you can change it. Yes, you can have happiness when you want it, more and more all the time, if you want it. Everything is an illusion and you can have what you want. EVERYONE CAN HAVE WHAT THEY WANT.

There is plenty to go around for all, and with this understanding and knowing, there is no need to take or steal from someone else. Yes, you can. Oh yes, you can.

Allow yourself to have it. Give yourself permission to have it. That is the other hard part, giving yourself permission. Figure out how you can give yourself permission. As you are thinking and figuring it out, keep it simple.

Keep everything simple.

More changes are on the way!

Chapter 11

THE PRINCIPLES OF MANIFESTING

When things are not going right, when they are not going your way, when they are not going the way you think they should be, you will need to adjust a couple of things within your state of functionality. In manifesting, no matter what you would like to manifest, there will be guidelines, principles, or rules you can follow — principles you can use to create a foundation for whatever it might be that you would like to manifest in, of, or for your life.

As you go along manifesting things in your life, principles will change, because the better you get at manifesting is when you will need to put into practice other principles, other rules that you will figure out and create for yourself. There are a few principles that I will share with you, which will be guidelines to begin. You might wish to write these down. If you have a very good memory, then you can memorize them. If not, you might want to write them down.

> # The Principles Of Manifesting: ™
>
> ## Think It   See It   Form It   Attract It
>
> ## Become It
>
> ## Allow It   Act It

Think It

When there is something you would like to have, create, or manifest in your life, you will begin by seeing it. How do you see something? What do you do to see it? First, you need to THINK IT. Once you think it, you can begin to see it. Since everything begins with thought, you will think what you want to manifest. How do you think? Usually, how do you think? At times, you might think clearly, or at times you might think with judgment. Sometimes you might think with desperation, or at times you might think with self-sabotage. Let's assume you think clearly and you don't involve yourself with judgment and all the rest. As you begin thinking clearly, you will think of what you want to create or manifest in your life. What do you do to think? Does thought require an emotion, or does thought create the emotion?

Really, it is a bit of both at the same time. What about desire? Where does desire come into play? When you think it, when you see it, you desire it at the same time. *Thinking is usually thinking, seeing, and desiring all at one time.*

Assuming there is something you want in your life, you will think about it. As you think about what you want, I would suggest you casually think about it. Don't do anything else but just casually think about what you want. If you can attach no emotion and just think about it, this would be a good thing. Emotion will come into play a bit later. Think about what you want and do it right now.

I am sure you have something you want in your life. Think about it. Just simply think about it. Attach nothing to it yet. Think of what it is, what it might be, what it could be, what it can be, and simply let it be. As you are thinking casually about what you want, think of one more thing; think of your life without it. Do nothing else. Just think of your life as being without it. Now, go back to thinking about it. Think about what you want in your life and do nothing, nothing but think about it. Have no response. Not yet. Have no emotion. Not yet. Have no desire. Not yet. Just think about what you want.

See It

As you are thinking, now begin to SEE IT in your mind, in your imagination. Begin seeing what you want. How can you see it? You can see it in any way you would like it to be. If you are seeing what you want, see it in a grand way. If you think small, you will be small. If you think in a GRAND way, you will be grand. If you see in a small way, you will have things in a small way. If you see those things in a grand way, you will have them in a grand way, so see what you are seeing in a grand way.

Take the thought of what you want and see it in the grandest way you can imagine it. Do not respond. Do not react. Do nothing. Just see it. You have thought it; now you are simply seeing it, and you are seeing it in a grand way, so use your imagination. Stretch your imagination more and more, and see what you want in a grand way. If it is something you want to do in or with your life, see yourself doing it in a grand way – the grandest way you can see it – and see it being done by you in the grandest way that it can be done by you. Do nothing else. Not yet. Just see it.

You have thought it in a grand way. You are now seeing it in a grand way. If you are having a problem seeing it in a grand way, or seeing it at all, it is all right. Eventually, you will see it. You will begin to see it. This is something that might take a bit of practice, so you have, and you will have, the principles that you can use over and over again, if you want to. The more you use them, the more proficient you will get at manifesting what you want.

Form It

Now, as you are seeing it in a grand way, begin to FORM IT in a grand way. You can have a thought. You can see something, but it may have no form. You will now begin to form it. What do you do to form something? You give it form, you give it reason, you give it meaning. What meaning will be in what you want, or what you want to do? What is the meaning? What does it mean to you? What can it mean to your life, your lifestyle, or your reality? Give it form. Form it in your imagination. Give it all form. Form it in the grandest way you can. Have no emotion. Do not react. Do not respond. Just form it. If it seems as though it is forming itself, then let it. If it seems as though it is forming itself in a different way than you would like it to, for now, let it, and observe the way that it is forming itself. What you should NOT be doing is forcing anything. Do not force anything. Just give it form. Form it in your imagination and remember to form it in a grand way.

Attract It

You have thought it, you have seen it, and you have formed it. Now, ATTRACT IT. With either your eyes closed or open—which will be up to you—gently, as you are forming it, gently begin to attract the energy to you. How do you attract energy to you? Remember and realize everything is energy. You are energy. To attract the energy to you of what you want, or what you want to do, all you need to do is realize that since everything is energy, including you, you need only desire it. How does desire differ from thinking, seeing, or forming? Now is when you will bring emotion into the picture. Desire is when you can form it with emotion. Once you begin to have emotion, maybe excitement, and maybe joy—once you have emotion, the energy of what you want will simply attract itself to you. You need do very little to attract what you want to you. You are energy. Your emotions are energy. Everything is energy. You will be merging yourself, your being, your consciousness, with the energy of what you want, or what you want to do. If it is something you want to do and you have seen it in a grand way, now use your emotion in a grand way. If you feel excitement, be excited in a grand way, not in a small way. Anything you do in a small way will keep things small for you. Anything you do in a grand way will let things be grand for you. Merge your energies with the energies of what you want or what you want to do. What do you need to do to merge your energies? You've been doing it. *Feel* the emotion *in* what you want and *of* what you want.

If you are forming something you want, remember to form it in your imagination in a grand way. See yourself doing it in the grandest way you can see yourself doing it. Everything will be in a grand way. Why? When everything is in a grand way, your emotions can only respond that way – in a grand way. If your emotions respond in a small way, then you have an issue to deal with – self-worth or fear. Self-worth is a big one. Many times people think, feel, or believe they do not deserve everything. I can tell you right now, that yes, you do deserve everything. You have created your life. You have created everything about your life. Certainly you deserve everything, and you always will deserve everything.

Fear is another big one, but really what is there to fear? Tell me, what is there to fear? The only thing to fear, when you think about it, is what you really don't yet understand. When you think of something, *see* that something, *form* that something, and *attract* that something. There is nothing that you don't or can't understand, because this is your creation. You are creating what you want and certainly you understand what you want, otherwise you wouldn't be able to create it. On the other hand, if you really think you don't understand something, all you need to do is begin creating it. As you do, then you will have a thorough understanding of what it is and why it is.

At this point, why do you want to create something? Why? The answer is simply because you *want* to create something. That is why. You do not need a reason why. I told you and I will tell you again. You have created your life. You have created everything in your life. You create simply because you want to create. This is why you are alive. To create. The purpose of being alive is to be creative, to do things in a grand way, and, of course, this is all based upon if you want to. If you want to.

At times, you might not want to create in a grand way. If you find those times when you do not want to create in a grand way, then look within yourself and you will usually find an emotion, or emotions, preventing you. What will they be all about? If you look at them with no judgment, and let them be what they are, they will reveal themselves to you, and they will tell you what they are all about and why they are. Then you will understand them. With understanding them, then you can change them, or get rid of them. You do not need to hold on to emotions that do not allow you to be GRAND. You do not need to hold on to emotions that hold you down or prevent you from doing something or having something. *You do not need them.* You do not need them. There is nothing that states that you need those emotions. Change them.

Since emotions are energy, then all emotions are equal. Fear then becomes equal with strength. Sadness becomes equal with joy. When you begin looking at emotions in that way, then everything becomes pure creative energy. Why? Because you have no *judgment* placed upon emotions, or energy, or anything.

As you are attracting what you want, or what you want to do, as you are feeling emotions in a grand way, do one thing for yourself right now. That one thing is to give yourself permission to have what you want. When you truly give yourself permission, you cannot have emotions that do not allow you to have what you want. It is impossible. It cannot be done. What do you need to do to give yourself permission? Think about your life. Who created your life? Here we go again—YOU. You have created everything in your life, and unconsciously you have given yourself permission to do so over and over again, keeping everything in a very, very, very simple state of being. Really, all you need to do is simply say with no judgment at all, "I give myself permission to have what I want. I give myself permission to do what I want to do, and to do it the way I want to do it, and to have it in the way I want to have it."

Giving yourself permission is a very, very, very simple and easy thing to do. You might believe you might not be able to give yourself permission having no judgment placed upon anything. This is something you might need to practice a few times. A good way to practice giving yourself permission is to go throughout your day, with everything you do, with everything you see, give yourself permission to do it. Give yourself permission to see it. "I give myself permission to do this, no matter how big or small it might be." Look at something; "I give myself permission to see this." This might sound silly, but this is a very good way to practice giving yourself permission.

Again, think of money. Many people have anxiety over money, fear about money, and desperation with the idea of money. When you have money be in its most simple form, and by that I mean with no judgment placed upon it, it is only just another idea. It is only energy. If what you want is money, then I might suggest you become *equal* with the idea of money.

If you want money, become equal with the idea of money.

Take your paper money, it does not matter how much you have, take it and place it all around your home so you can see it—every time you look somewhere, you will see it. It just might become boring. This is a good thing. To have it become boring means the importance, the anxiety, is falling away. Now, if you want something else, or if you are trying to do something, or if you want to do something, then everyday for a few seconds time, see yourself doing it in your imagination in a grand way, or see what you want in your life in a grand way, and let it go.

Become It

You have thought it, you have seen it, you have formed it, you have attracted it, and now you will BECOME IT. What you want to do or what you want, you will become it. So maybe there is something you want—a new automobile. How in the world can you become an automobile? It is a very easy thing to do. Remember energy. Remember everything is energy, so you will become the energy of the automobile, or whatever it is you want. You will become the energy of what you want to do. How do you become the energy? *You feel what you want inside of you.* Remember the excitement. It is within the excitement. You feel what you want inside of you, inside of your body. Feel the energy inside your body. If it is a new automobile, use your imagination in a grand way, the grandest way you can, and feel the energy of the automobile inside your body. Imagine it, because everything is imagination. Imagine the energy of the automobile is inside your body. Feel it. Feel it within you.

If you want to do something in your life, or with your life, feel the energy of you doing it now. Feel the energy of doing it *now.* Don't think, don't say, and don't believe that you will do it later. Don't think, don't feel, and don't believe that you will have what you want at a later time. If you think, feel, or believe that way, it will always be at a later time. You will become what you want. You will become what you want to do. *You will become the energies of all of that now.* Feel the energies within you NOW.

As you are feeling the energies within you, think how things are right now. Since you have become the energies of what you want, or what you want to do, see how your life has changed *now*. How has it changed? You will see it change. You will notice a change. Why? Because your reality is your emotional energy. It is your thought energy. When you excite yourself you excite your reality.

> **You will become the energy of what you want to do. How do you become the energy? You FEEL what you want inside of you.**

When your emotions change within you, when your thoughts change within you, your reality will also change according to your emotions and your thoughts. Become the energy of what you want, or what you want to do, and become it NOW. You have what you want now. Imagine it that way. Think it that way. See it that way. Form it that way. You have attracted it. It is now. It is all NOW, and what you want to do is feel yourself — feel yourself doing it now. See yourself doing it now. Think that you are doing it now. Form it so you are doing it now. You have attracted it to you, so you are doing it NOW.

> **When your emotions change within you, when your thoughts change within you, your reality will also change according to your emotions and your thoughts.**

Don't forget to do it in a grand way, or have what you want in a grand way. Keep everything in a grand way. Have nothing in a small way. You are a very, very creative individual. You might not think it, you might not know it, and you might not realize it until you try yourself out at creating.

If you seem to make mistakes, remember that mistakes or failures are only more successes that you create, because they tell you, teach you, or show you, how to do the same things in a different way. You may need to take the same idea that you have, or what you want, or what you want to do, and you may need to, or you might want to, do the same thing in many different ways. The longer you persist at something, the sooner you will have that something. Remember—not in a desperate way.

This really does make sense. When you focus on something, you will create it. What is focusing? *Focusing is giving something an intention.* What you intend for your life, what you intend to do, you will have for your life, or you will do it. Focus your attention on what you want or what you want to do.

Think it, see it, form it, attract it, focus your attention, and with your focus of attention, you will be creating intention. *Everything has intention* or it would not exist in your reality. When things do not have intention, they might just exist in your dream state, in which you will give them intention. Then at one point or another, they will create themselves. They will manifest in, or as a part of, your physical reality.

Allow It

You have thought it, you have seen it, you have formed it, you have attracted it, and you have become it. Now comes the big one. You will now ALLOW IT. You will now allow it. Let me see, what does it mean to allow something? It means accepting it the way it is. You will not put anything on it. You will not emotionally charge it one way or the other way. You will not judge it.

Certainly, you will not judge it. If you judge something, you cannot allow it; you cannot allow it to be as it is. When you judge it, you will change it within its own frequency, within its own foundation, within its own structure. It will change when you judge it, then you will not have what you want to have. You will not do what you want to do. So, you will allow it. You will put nothing on it. You will not judge it. You will let it be the way it is, and you will let it be for what it is.

When you are allowing something, you might think to yourself, "All right, I can allow this. I am allowing this. I am not judging it. I am not putting anything on it. I am not charging it with any kind of energy, but how do I really know it will manifest itself?" How do you really know anything will manifest itself? How do you really know? How do you really know anything? You know anything and you know everything, and you know how and when things will manifest, because you will tell them when and how to manifest with no judgment, no charge, with nothing. You are telling things how and when to manifest your intention. It is your intention.

How do you know you are alive? How do you know you breathe? You simply know it. You don't sit and think, "Well, here are all the ways that tell me I'm alive. Here are all the things, all the ideas that tell me I'm breathing." You don't think that way. You don't even think about it. You simply know it. You know you are alive. You know you are breathing. You know everything you do, or you wouldn't do it. You know everything you do, so it follows then, you know how to create. You know everything you create. You know how to manifest. You know everything you manifest. Look around you. You've created everything you see. You've allowed and given yourself permission to manifest everything you see. You had thought it, seen it, formed it, attracted it, you have become it, and you had allowed it.

Your reality is consciousness. Your reality has consciousness. It knows what to do when you quit fighting your reality, and I am not saying that you are, but when you quit fighting reality, it will perform more brilliantly for you. The purpose of reality is to serve you, to give you what you want. Reality is your playground. It is where, and it is when, you play with your ideas and create them, and it is where, and it is when, you imagine your ideas and you manifest them.

> **Your reality has consciousness. It knows what to do. When you quit fighting your reality, it will perform more brilliantly for you. The purpose of reality is to serve you, to give you what you want.**

Reality, once you allow it to be in its most simple form, will work brilliantly for you. It will serve you in magnificent ways, and all you need to do is leave it alone and let it do what it knows how to do. I am not telling you that if you want a brand new automobile all you have to do is think it, see it, form it, attract it, become it, and allow it, and you will have it. No, there is a bit more to it than that.

Act it

There is the idea of action, which can be one more principle you can use for now. ACT IT. Action is something that you might need to practice a few times to get the hang of it, and once you do, action will become second nature to you. It will be something you do without even thinking about it, seeing it, forming it, attracting it to you, or anything else. You will simply be in a state of action all the time. This is what you want, if you want to manifest. When you take action, act also in a grand way, because if you think grand, see grand, form grand, attract grand, and all the rest, in a grand way, you will create everything in a grand way. If you act in a small way, you will take everything down to a small form.

I am not telling you to mount a white steed and parade down the streets of your town in a grand way. No. As you are going throughout your life, day-to-day, be grand. Be grand about everything. Do nothing in a small way. Do everything in a grand way. I think you understand what I am telling you. There is a difference between doing things in a grand way and doing things in a small way, and if you think about the difference, you will know exactly what I am telling you.

When you feel good, you do things in a good way. When you are feeling slow, or low of energy, you tend to do things in a small way. Oh, by the way, you can never be low of energy. At times, you can be lazy, and if you find yourself being lazy, it is all right for a time. Give yourself a time limit. Be lazy for one and one-half days, or two days, then see yourself, think of yourself, form yourself taking action again — action in a grand way. Act in a grand way. Walk in a grand way. Talk in a grand way. Don't be egotistical. Don't be obnoxious. Be confident, be sure, and be knowing. *This is acting in a grand way — confidence, sureness, and knowing.* This is acting in a grand way. You have done this before many times throughout your life. You will do it again many times during the rest of your life. Now is the time to be conscious of doing it.

Many times, you have acted in a grand way unconsciously, not knowing what you were doing, but for some reason, things worked out, things began to work for you. It might be a miracle. No, you are the miracle. You are THE only miracle. All of those things that you create, that you think might be a miracle, are things you have created in your own image by acting in a grand way. From now on be, or at least try to be, consciously aware of acting in a grand way, and again, don't be egotistical, don't be obnoxious. Be confident, sure, and knowing.

As you begin to manifest all of these principles and rules, the guidelines will change for you. This is something you can start with, something you can begin with, and by you being the creator of your own reality, you will create and recreate principles of manifesting, rules of manifesting, guidelines of, and for, manifesting, for the rest of your lifetime.

You will need to do that, because you will manifest and create more, and more, and more in a grand way. As you do so, the principles must change. They must change to keep up with you and you will change them. You will restructure them, and you will manifest and create more in a very grand way.

> **All you have to do to have all this work for you is to just DO IT. Very simple: DO IT. If it excites you, DO IT. If you fear it, DO IT EVEN MORE.**

All you have to do—all you have to do to have all this work for you—is just to DO IT. Very simple: DO IT. If it excites you, do it. If you fear it, do it even more. Remember, emotions are energy. They are all equal. Fear can be excitement when you let it be. Let it be.

Let your thoughts be. Let your reality be, and let yourself be grand. Let yourself be grand, because when you do anything, you can do anything in a grand way and when you do anything, you can really do everything. You *can* really do everything.

I have said it before and I will say it again; *all you need to do to have all this work for you is to DO IT.* Just do it. A very easy thing to do. Just do it.

Chapter 12

GOAL PLANNING

How do you feel about your life? How do you feel about your goals for your life? Do you have goals for, and in, your life? Have you considered them? Have you thought them through? Do you have a plan for them? Do you have a theme for them? What is your biggest goal? Waking up in the morning? Not feeling pain? Creating inventions? Creating more business opportunities? More joy in the day? Expanding your career? Helping people find out who they are? Undecided?

Your biggest goal is your life. That is your biggest goal. All other goals are a part of that—a part of your life. Your life is your identity, so your number one primary goal should really be changing facets of your identity so you can settle within your own self and truly be what you want to accomplish in, and with, your life.

> **Your biggest goal is your life. All other goals are only a part of your life.**

You will go throughout your life trying this and that goal, deciding this and that idea, and many times hoping they will work out. If you were to establish yourself within your identity and change your identity, then you wouldn't have to try anything, then you would just be doing and accomplishing everything. At this very moment, how do you feel about yourself, your life, and your lifestyle?

Now think of how you feel about your creative side, your creative self. Is it really functioning to the best of its ability, or is there room for improvement? Think about your lifestyle. Are you living precisely the lifestyle that you would like to live? Think about your ability and your willingness to accomplish all ideas and goals in your life. Are you really allowing yourself enough creative freedom to accomplish all your ideas and goals, or is something holding you back? If there is something holding you back, think what it might be. Your answer probably will be, "myself." If that is your answer, you are right. If your answer is something outside of you, like a circumstance or situation, you are wrong.

As I have said many times, and I will again refresh your memory, *it all begins within you as it all ends within you, and an ending is only a new beginning.*

When you consider goal planning, you must first consider yourself. Consider yourself as being the supreme force of your life — the supreme force of your life. The creative god in your life, because that is what you are. Begin thinking of yourself in that way. You *are* the supreme force of your life and you are also *the* creative god in your life. When you can think of yourself in that way, you will then find the freedom to change your identity, and to establish yourself within your identity.

> **You are the supreme force of your life and you are also the creative god in your life.**

Having Identity

You have goals, ideas, and things you would like to set into motion, things you would like to accomplish in this lifetime. It is good to have ideas and goals, but it is better when you have identity. You know yourself to be what you are and how you are right now.

If you can slightly change that and create a shift in your identity as well as your thinking, then you will become someone else *within* your being; that someone else will be about freedom and willingness to *allow* all things to become manifest in this physical lifetime. When you have an idea or goal, many times you will begin its manifestation by thinking it over and choosing how you would like it to end and become a part of your reality.

Step 1: Feel The Energy of Your Goal

Seldom will you think about the first step first and allow yourself to enjoy all the steps necessary in creating your goals. Too many times, you will consider the end result first, and when you do, that will bring up many issues within you. "What if something goes wrong? What if it doesn't work out?"

Think over your goal or idea and feel its energy. Simply feel its energy. Ask the energy of your goal, or idea, what is the first step you need to do, or take, to allow it to accomplish itself in your reality. It will tell you. It may tell you to first settle yourself down, give up your anxiety and desperation, and *become* the energy. How do you become the energy of your idea or goal? It is very simple. You *feel* the energy of your idea or goal. You can do it. You have done it countless times without realizing what you are doing. Feel the energy within your body, within your being, and then think of yourself in that way. In other words, think of yourself as *being your goal*, because you *are* your goal. It is your creation, which means it is a part of you and part of your identity.

Step 2: Define Your Intention

Once you can *feel* the energy, and once you can *become* the energy, then think of your intention for creating your idea or goal. Why do you wish its creation and manifestation? Why? What does it mean to you? What does it mean to you to manifest your idea or goal? It does have a meaning, so think about the meaning.

In thinking about your idea or goal, and feeling the energy, and becoming the energy, then remind yourself that since it is your creation and part of your identity. Nothing, or no one, can hold you back or hold you down from accomplishing your idea or goal.

Step 3: Ask The Energy What to Do And Write It Down

When you get that far, and when you have asked the energy of your idea or goal what you should do first, then write down on paper with a pencil the steps you will take to create your goal. When you have written down all your steps that you will get from asking the energy what you should do to allow it is manifestation, then you will begin to create a theme for your goal.

Step 4: Create A Theme For Your Goal

A theme is a topic or subject matter, if you don't already know this. All things in your life, and lifestyle, will have a theme. With *all* things in your life, there is a theme. These themes may be shared or different from each other, and they each have something unique about them. Think of all the *things* in your life and all the people in your life, and lifestyle, and when you think about them, you will understand and realize that each will have its own special identity.

To create a theme for your goal, you will give it an identity. Perfection is a theme; accomplishment, success, failure, freedom, allowance, acceptance, and judgment are themes. Holding yourself back is a theme, and your own lifestyle has its own theme. Your identity has its own theme also. When you are considering your goal, and after writing down all your steps, give it its own theme and identity.

You do the same thing in, and about, your day every day and in your own way. How you are and what you do is your theme. When you figure out the purpose of your goal, then you can give it a theme. Its purpose will become its theme. When you look around at all you have created so far in your life you will begin to understand how each different thing, situation, or individual will have its own theme. Begin by looking around you and look within your life, and lifestyle, and begin to understand all your themes. When you have figured out what your lifestyle theme is, then you can change it, if you wish to.

Usually you will find there is something within your lifestyle theme that needs a shift and a change. Once you give yourself permission to allow for the change to take place, all you have to do is say to yourself, "This is going to change and I will allow the change."

Once you do that, it has been done, and there is nothing else you have to do but allow it to be in a new way. I do much talking about doing things in a new way. By now, I think you know what I mean by that. If you choose not to, it is all right. Remember though, if what you are doing is not working for you, do it again. Begin again in a new and different way, with a new intention.

Begin again by asking yourself why you want to do it, what is its purpose, and what does it mean for you in your life and to your life. Maybe you will want to change its purpose or meaning. If the purpose is to create a wealth of money, and should you have a fear of money, maybe you would like to have its purpose be to help people, which will take the pressure off you and your belief about money. Many people have a fear of money. People enjoy money, but they fear it. It comes, it goes, and for some, it never stays. Why? Because people don't understand the game of money. Money has its own theme, and it is its own game. People don't understand what money means, how to manage money, create money, and how to enjoy money. Most people *think* they know how to enjoy money, but not really. When you have a fear of something, you will usually have little enjoyment attached to it unless you really enjoy being in fear of it. Then fear becomes excitement. It is only energy—nothing more and nothing less than energy, as is your idea or goal, as is your identity and your lifestyle.

Your lifestyle is an understanding of yourself and how your lifestyle is, and precisely how you understand yourself at this precise moment. Would you like or change your lifestyle, how you understand yourself, and understand yourself in a different way?

"How can I do that?"

I will tell you. When you do something in a different way, a shift takes place, and a change takes place within your conscious mind, which causes a change to take place in your identity. When that takes place, you will have a new understanding about yourself. You usually understand yourself in very limited ways, and there are many ways to understand yourself, because you are what? You are multidimensional.

Now, I am about to use the words "level and levels" to make a point. I don't care for these words when talking about the mind, consciousness, and being, because there are no "levels" to the self. So, here we go. Being multidimensional means there are many levels within, and to, your being. There are levels within your conscious mind, levels within, and to, your unconscious and subconscious mind, and that is why, many times, you will create dreams in which you are acting out a situation or a problem that is taking place in your life at that time. You will experience yourself within many levels of your own self, and you do this all the time. You function within, and from, all of your levels all the time. Even when you consider yourself to be highly focused on something, you are focused within many levels of your being or your awareness. So when you consider your goals, realize your goals have awareness, because they are your thoughts, and thoughts are energy. When you truly understand that all things are energy, then it will become quite apparent to you that not only are all things your creations, but they are also your accomplishments, and that will lead you to understand that all you have created is what you are.

You Are Always Equal To Your Goals

Many times, you will consider your goals to be larger and grander than you. Quit thinking that way, and understand and realize they are your creations, and that makes you equal with them. You are only and always equal to your goals. Let me repeat this. *You are only and always equal to your goals.*

You have attachments to your ideas and goals, because they are a part of you, and each will have its own meaning. Ask your ideas and goals what meaning they have in, and for, your life and they will tell you. Don't confuse your goals within yourself, because many times, when a person considers goals in, or for, his or her life, he or she will begin to confuse the goals, because one will lead into another one. One will take you into another one. Then you will ask yourself, "What am I doing and where should I begin? Things are changing and I don't know what I am doing anymore."

It is a good idea to focus on one goal at a time for a short time. You do not need to focus and meditate, meditate and focus, focus and meditate for long periods of time. Three minutes is enough time to consider your goal, and at the end of three minutes you will have established the goal's identity, the goal's theme, and the goal's purpose and meaning for your life. Then the energies will be set into your reality and will have become a part of your lifestyle. Do you understand me? At this moment in time, how are you now thinking of your goals—the same or a bit differently? Why, and in what way?

Take Action

Action—yes, indeed, you do need to take action. It would be very nice to sit and think, and think, and think, and focus, and think, and hope, and wish, and have all things manifest. Sorry, but physical life is not that way. You need to take action. When you have established the theme for your goal, which means reason, purpose, and identity, then you can begin to take action.

Let's go back to money for a moment. Think of yourself as being so wealthy you don't even know how much money you have available to you. How does that feel? Think again. How does it really feel? Out of control? Think of your finances as they are right now. I would bet they are a bit out of control. Right or wrong? If your answer is no, they are not out of control, then congratulations, you have created and established all that you would like in, of, and for your life.

Sometimes people have enough money by doing things they don't want to do, and sometimes people keep jobs they hate just because the money is good. People will rationalize and justify this with the notion that doing things they do not want to do will allow them to do what they want to do. Really? To that, I say hogwash! It doesn't have to be like that. If you had the opportunity, and you had the opportunity right now, to do what you really want to do, would you do it? Yes or no? Why? How does it make you feel when you think about doing what you really want to do? If you had the opportunity, if you had the opportunity, if you had the opportunity—do you know where I am going with this?

You DO have the opportunity. Since you DO have the opportunity, why do you still believe you should or must do what you do not want to do, so that in time you can do what you want to do? Why do you believe that? I will tell you why. *Because society teaches you that.* Society teaches people they have to work hard and do things they do not want to do to get what they want.

Let's say you have a job you do not like which pays the bills and gives you money so you can do what you want on the side, and eventually make your goal a reality. Let's also say things don't ever come to fruition or there are missed opportunities, and at times, you are thankful you never quit your day job to pursue your goal. Why do you think things have not worked out? Maybe because a part of you isn't ready for it.

You may experience a plethora of thoughts and emotions analyzing why.

"Well, I look at why all the time. I question it, I try so many different things from the forceful push to I'll just relax and let it come. I try so many gamuts. I question myself and ask why I am in the same dream, day after day, after day, and I am not able to just create it the way I want—maybe my awareness alone is changing it, and many times, it feels like I am almost there and I feel it. I really feel it, and it's not there. It doesn't happen. Do I really feel I don't deserve it?"

Everyone experiences this, and this may ring true for you. Every day, people do this. There must be something, or someone within you who is telling you that you really don't deserve that yet, and you must wait before you do deserve that.

"I'll tell you when you can have it, and you must wait before you deserve that, and I'll tell you when you deserve that, and in the meantime I'll let you come close to it, but not have it. I will dictate to you when you can have it and how much of it you can have." So, what do you think that something, or someone is within you?

It's your identity and your theme as it is right now.

If it is true for you, and if it is your identity, then what do you need to do?

"Change my identity?"

Change it in what way?

"By taking a look at it?"

Exactly. By taking a look at it, you change it. When you look at and consider something, you are changing what you are looking at or considering, which is the way energy works. When you consider it, it will change.

"I've done everything I can think of. I am knocking myself out and I am tired of thinking of what I can do to create what I want for, and in, my life. I think, and I try, and I do, and I think, try, and do again. I meditate, I focus, I visualize, I meditate, focus, and visualize, and I think, and I think, and I do. I think, I try, I do. I'll try again. I'll think again even though I know it'll be the same, but I'll do it anyway because I think somehow if I try hard and long enough it might take place my way. I feel frustrated, but I'll keep doing it anyway. I'll visualize ... oh, that looks nice. I can see it, I can feel it, it is becoming me, it is gone past me ... WHY?"

It Is All Your Belief About Yourself

It all has to do with how you believe about yourself. What you have been taught throughout your life is hiding and lurking in your unconscious and subconscious mind. Every chance they have, they will get you and "they" refers to all the things you have learned in your life. You have learned how to fail and you have also learned how to succeed, but many times learning how to fail will come first, and that will leave a lasting impression upon and within you.

We will discuss the issues again of success and failure. You know now how to create a theme for your goals. Right? You also know your goals are you. Right? You also know you need to become the energy of your idea or goal. Right? You now know how to do that. Right? I'll remind you.

When you feel the energy of your idea or goal, it will become part of your identity, and then all you need to do is allow yourself to begin acting as your idea or goal. If your goal is wealth, then begin acting as if you have wealth. It can be money, or health, or anything. Now you know how to do that. You also know you need to write down all the steps necessary in the creation of your goal. Let me remind you how to do that.

You ask the energy of your idea or your goal what you need to do to allow it to become manifest in your reality, and it will tell you. Talk to the energy, or maybe you would like to see the energy as being a person. If you do, create a form or shape for your idea or your goal. See it as an individual and talk with it. It will answer you and tell you precisely what you need to do to have it manifest as a part of your reality.

Success and Failure

You know how to fail better than to succeed, which is all right, because now you will have the opportunity to change all that forever by knowing that all your failures *have been,* and *are,* successes within their own right. Every time you fail at something, you are allowing yourself the opportunity to see something new about yourself all over again. Why did you fail at something? Asking yourself that question will bring you an answer. It is all so simple. When you ask, you shall receive. It is as simple as that.

"Why did I fail with that idea? Oh, I am getting it now. I didn't believe I could create that idea. Oh wait, I am getting something new ... I believe I am not worthy of complete and total success. Oh, something else is coming at me ... I have been told throughout my life I can only achieve certain things and I shouldn't try other things, because they are not for me, but for someone else, so I should just do what I must do. What if I ask and I listen and I don't hear anything?"

When you truly listen, you will hear, and you truly must listen to yourself, because within yourself is ALL knowledge about and for yourself and your life. You have everything you need to know about yourself and your life within you right now and always. Since failures are really successes, the only thing in your life is success, no matter what you have done, no matter what you are doing, or trying to do. You *are* a success right now. Thinking of yourself in that way will *allow* you to begin *feeling* that way, and when you can feel like a success, you will become that success. *When you think, you are placing into motion energies about yourself, about your life, about your lifestyle, and about your reality.* The energies are working for you. They're building and growing within themselves to create what you want, and you must allow them to do their job.

> **When you think, you are placing into motion energies about yourself, about your life, about your lifestyle, and about your reality.**

Do not negate your ideas or goals with thoughts that state things might not work out. If self-defeating thoughts come up, rethink your original thought or your goal, or what you want to do, or what you will do. If that negative internal dialog insidiously creeps in, remind yourself that all failure is a success, and you are a success right now. You should also know that all your ideas and goals are easy to create once, and when, you allow them to function with, and within, their identity and their theme. Allow your old stories to fall away. You no longer need them.

Thinking of a goal or an idea will present many other thoughts to you. If you have thoughts of failing, simply say to yourself, "So what." That will

221

take away the importance of failing. Things in life are really so very simple, and if you can keep all things simple in life, you will recognize success, upon success, upon success, all the time—each and every day. Each and every day.

There are no failures. There are only and just successes, one after the next, when you think that way about yourself. You will see things change in your life. You will see it, because things will change and you will see the change. Money is energy. It is just an idea.

There is nothing to fear, unless you have placed judgment upon your worthiness. You truly deserve everything in life, you really do, and deep down within you, you know that. Maybe you would like to remind yourself of that a few times a day.

"Hey, wait a minute. I do deserve everything and when I hear those voices telling to me that I don't deserve everything, I'll say back to those voices, hogwash! You don't know what you are talking about. Go away thank you."

All of those voices will be your life's training. You have been taught, to a degree, you can have certain things, and you have been taught, to a degree, you do not deserve certain things. It is all right. You can change it by reminding yourself that you do deserve everything. Why? *Because all things are your creation.*

Get Excited

When you are in the thick of goal planning, there is the issue of excitement, which can be threatening to many people. Too many times, you will think of a goal in this way:

"I would really like to do that, and it would feel good and nice if I could to do that. I think I'll try it. I am not seeing it, but I'll try it when no one is around just in case it doesn't work, and I look stupid."

What is another way to think of your goals and how can you act it out? When you think about a goal, have EXCITEMENT ABOUT THE GOAL. All right? When you have anxiety, this is how you will think of your goal:

"I just have to do that. I just *have* to do it. If I don't, I'll just die. It means my entire life."

Are you hearing me? Thinking of your goal with excitement sounds like this:

"Hot damn, I'm going to do it. This is the new me ... hot damn, I'm going to do it." It is all in how you think. Your thoughts create your reality and all that resides within it. Your thoughts make you what you are, how you are, and why you are. Your thoughts do the same for your life and your lifestyle. Consider your lifestyle, and whether or not you would like to change it. If you do, change it. It is just that simple, so allow it to change.

Tell yourself frequently, "I now give my lifestyle the freedom to change and become what I truly deserve."

Once you do that, it has already begun. It has been done. When you think and when you verbalize your thoughts, you are charging your reality with the energy of your thought, or your desire, or your goal. When you need to accomplish your goal, or it is a job, a horrendous task that you must do, where is the joy? In this way of thinking, there is no joy or appreciation for yourself. All the things you need to do, simply *want* to do them and put excitement into it.

"I can do it and I will."

If your excitement changes from day to day, so what. You will change with each moment of time throughout your life, and you will change each day. Your thoughts, your moods, and your emotions will change each day. So what. Let them.

Listen closely to me. Do not attempt to create when you doubt yourself or when you are not feeling excitement about your goal. If you do, you will create your goal, but it might be like a wet noodle. It will then mean very little to you. Its theme might be boredom. If you are working with a group, a mastermind group, make sure everyone is on the same page concerning the theme of the goal, otherwise it will become a competition.

So, now you have goal planning mastered. Right? When you have a goal in mind, you will have excitement. Right? You will ask its energy what you should do to allow it its freedom to create itself, and you will listen. Right? You will write down the steps. Right? You will feel the energy. Right? You will become the energy. Right? Sometimes you will fail. Right? So what if you do. When you do fail, think of your failure as a success, because it is showing and teaching you something new about yourself, namely what you shouldn't do again.

THERE IS NO FAILURE, ONLY CREATIVE OPPORTUNITY.

DON'T TRY.

DO.

A PERSONAL NOTE FROM TOM MASSARI

B y the time I was 15, music was my life and my world. My first band, The Apocryphals, was one of the top bands in Chicago, Illinois, by the mid-60s, which is when I ranked sixth best drummer in a citywide competition. Unfortunately, the band broke up at the end of the decade and I moved to California as a member of another band.

By 1973, I found myself back in the Midwest, living in Milwaukee, Wisconsin, where my life took a surprising and unexpected turn. I became involved in metaphysics due to some paranormal experiences in California, and I opened the Parapsychology Center where ESP development, hypnosis, and meditation were taught. This is when I met Sue, my current wife.

My involvement in meditation led me to compose my first meditation CD entitled *Focal Point Alpha Meditation,* which was widely sold in the United States for several years to metaphysical book stores, massage therapists, and acupuncturists, and still is being sold to this day! Since the Focal *Point Alpha Meditation,* I have composed a number of meditation and sleep CD's, music for a motion picture soundtrack, and several jazz-rock albums.

In 1977, I moved back to California, continued my involvement in metaphysics, and lost touch with Sue for over thirty years. By the time we reconnected in 2008, by way of the Internet, I was living in Arizona, and the rest is history. Sue and I each have our unique spiritual gifts and talents, and with our other creative endeavors, such as my music and Sue's writing, artistic interests, and psychic mediumship development, we have a deep desire to serve humanity and offer people a fresh way of seeing themselves and the life they create.

We hope you have enjoyed the book, and at the very least, allowed it to stir your imagination and question your own set of beliefs.

A PERSONAL NOTE FROM SUE MASSARI

In 1973 I found my way to the Parapsychology Center in Milwaukee, Wisconsin, eager to learn more about ESP and the world of spirit. It was a relief to be able to openly talk about my life-long psychic experiences, and I had no idea what was in store for me when I met Tom.

After Tom moved to California and I lost touch with him, I eventually moved to Seattle, Washington, where I looked for another group of like-minded people. I quickly abandoned my search after finding little authenticity in the psychic field. Metaphysics in the 70's was not openly accepted like it is today, so I studied on my own and continued my life, often putting metaphysics on the back burner.

Things really started to rev up psychically in the 90's when my focus and connection with people in spirit became a priority. To be honest with you, it scared me. Throughout my life when I would feel energy around me and get visions of people, I thought I was just getting psychic impressions never knowing I could communicate with spirit, and I had no idea what mediumship was or how to develop it.

After reading numerous books over the years, I found most belief systems were not for me, and I felt little connection with the "New Age" movement. I wanted knowledge that was ageless, timeless, and practical that I could use to truly evolve my soul. Tom's ability was hard to top and my introduction to channeling was from one of the best.

Happily, things changed in 2002 when I found a woman teaching mediumship development a few hours from my home in Florida. Although I didn't agree with many things she taught, it did give me a foundation from which to work, and once I better understood my experiences I took the ball and ran with it on my own.

Understanding that we create and are responsible for our own reality can be a little unsettling if one is not used to thinking and living their life from that perspective. Abram gently guides and encourages people to understand themselves in a much broader way so we can achieve greatness as individuals and as a race of beings.

Abram's knowledge and advice has been enlightening and inspiring. I am very blessed to have him as my mentor and part of my life experience.

CPSIA information can be obtained
at www.ICGtesting.com
Printed in the USA
FFHW011435120219
49398611-55774FF